One Man's
Miracles

One Man's
Miracles

Kevin Stroud

A Division of WINEPRESS PUBLISHING

© 2007 by Kevin Stroud. All rights reserved.

Pleasant Word (a division of WinePress Publishing, PO Box 428, Enumclaw, WA 98022) functions only as book publisher. As such, the ultimate design, content, editorial accuracy, and views expressed or implied in this work are those of the author.

No part of this publication may be reproduced, stored in a retrieval system, or transmitted in any way by any means—electronic, mechanical, photocopy, recording, or otherwise—without the prior permission of the copyright holder, except as provided by USA copyright law.

Unless otherwise noted, all Scriptures are taken from the *Holy Bible, New International Version®*, NIV®. Copyright © 1973, 1978, 1984 by the International Bible Society. Used by permission of Zondervan. All rights reserved.

Scripture references marked KJV are taken from the King James Version of the Bible.

Scripture references marked NASB are taken from the New American Standard Bible, © 1960, 1963, 1968, 1971, 1972, 1973, 1975, 1977 by The Lockman Foundation. Used by permission.

ISBN 13: 978-1-4141-1029-5
ISBN 10: 1-4141-1029-4
Library of Congress Catalog Card Number: 2007904183

Table of Contents

Preface vii

Miracle One: The Drowning 9
Miracle Two: Kathy to the Rescue 19
Miracle Three: The Propeller 37
Miracle Four: Births 47
Miracle Five: Jennifer's Dive 57
Miracle Six: Kathy to the Rescue Part II 63
Miracle Seven: Emergency Leave 75
Miracle Eight: Katherine's Farewell 83
Miracle Nine: Stephanie's Shocker 91
Miracle Ten: This Book 107
Miracle Eleven: Salvation 123

Preface

This book does not seek to highlight any specific events in my life. I am not someone famous, or anyone who has done anything particularly special to the point where people other than my family and friends would be interested in reading about.

This book is a highlight of some of God's miracles in my life. Everyone has stories like these and should be able to find many more such events. Many go through life calling these events "lucky" or "coincidence." Well, if that were the case, an awful lot of luck or coincidence has gone on in just my life. When you stop to think of the similar stories (and much greater stories of such "luck" and "coincidence") that each of the nearly 6.5 billion people on earth has experienced, you come to realize that all that luck and coincidence are miracles.

As you read, I give you insight into my thought process at the time. Some of you will read things I say, especially relating to the Bible and God, and feel that some of it just isn't right. I've grown, and will continue to grow, as a Christian, but I wanted to explain my thought process at that time, because I think it illustrates just how patient God has been with me.

God is speaking to us through the miracles he performs in all of our lives. He is here and he loves you.

Miracle One

The Drowning

In your distress you called and I rescued you...
—Psalm 81:7

One weekend during my seventh grade, my friend's mom decided to rent a cabin at Merrimac State Park in Missouri. Eight boys, all thirteen-year-olds, were beginning to feel they needed to assert their right to have independence by rebelling against the rules their parents had set for them. It was a weekend of first time smoking, drinking beer, taking a puff of marijuana, and even a midnight streaking run through the crowded campground. It was 1975, after all, and we were spending a whole weekend largely unsupervised.

For her part, Mrs. Jackson wanted a quiet get-away-from-it-all experience. I do not even remember seeing her there the whole weekend. I don't know if she never left her room, or was just always asleep when we returned in the early morning hours and already out when we awoke. To give us this kind of freedom, she was the coolest mom we had ever seen. Anyway, her son Vic had earned the right to be one of the leaders of our wild gang by getting us here on this freedom weekend.

We arrived early in the evening on a Friday night, and after throwing our bags on the bunks we all headed out to the trails with our flashlights. We joked, explored, and took turns hassling each other well after midnight. I was a tall kid, well above most of the other boys. George, who later became a star member of our junior high football team as a fullback, was about the same height as me, but a good fifty pounds heavier and already mostly muscle. I was what you'd call a lanky kid, tall and skinny as a rail. I was developing a bad case of acne, which I was extremely self-conscious about. Kids, being the socially responsible beings they are, teased about my "pizza face" regularly. Gary and Mickey were both popular with the girls and therefore were the natural leaders of our band. Me, George, Mike, Johnny, and Tim largely followed the "games" of Gary, Mickey, and Vic.

Even after our late night, we were up at daybreak and ready to do some fishing. Everyone grabbed their gear and began the three-quarter mile hike to the river. The woods were so peaceful and scenic—a stark contrast to the concrete jungle of our homes in St. Louis. We came out of the woods on a large boulder about fifteen feet above the Merrimac River. It was the prettiest river I had ever seen, emerald green and swiftly moving. We all sat there on the boulder for quite some time in silent reverence to the scenic beauty of the area. You could see little whirlpools float by that appeared as if the water was being stirred by hundreds of unseen hands. We were the only people in sight, and to us "city boys," it felt as if we were in paradise.

We tried a couple casts into the river, but the current was too swift for the lines. It wasn't but about fifteen minutes before we gave up on fishing for the rest of the trip. Besides,

The Drowning

there were many more exciting (and certainly less acceptable to our parents) adventures to live.

"Let's go swimming," someone suggested. I looked out at the swirling river and felt nervous, even though I was a fairly strong swimmer.

Splash! Gary was the first to jump. He dove head first into the river and quickly swam back to the left side of the boulder. It was more of a guided float, as the river quickly pushed him downstream. Gary was usually the first to do things, which was another reason why he was one of the leaders. Soon we were all jumping and diving into the river from that magnificent boulder and were quite happy for about half an hour.

"Let's swim to the other side of the river," Mickey suggested. He was the smallest of the group, but he got his leadership position by being one of the best jocks in the bunch.

We argued about this for awhile. The current looked awfully swift, and if you didn't make it across before you were taken downstream about a hundred yards, you would meet with a sheer cliff wall and be unable to get out. The current even picked up speed at that point with churning rapids clearly visible in the distance.

After numerous dares and double-dares, George dove and began swimming. We all anxiously watched as he made it across with plenty of room to spare. One after another we took turns. I went third and swam for all I was worth. I was scared the whole way, but had put in more effort than needed and made it across with less downstream movement than anyone else.

Gary went last. While he was the brave one who dove in first, he was the most nervous about trying to swim across and had said he wasn't going to do it. Well, now that everyone else had, and was calling on the "wimp" to

One Man's Miracles

come on, he dove and began swimming. He looked as if he was swimming OK, but the current was taking him quickly downstream. He was past us and already into the rock face when he was only about halfway across. We watched and screamed after him as he struggled to stay afloat. We could barely see him as he entered the rapids, and then he was out of sight.

"Let's go!" George hollered. George only took command when situations warranted it. He knew he was the strongest and Gary needed help. He started to go back across but quickly stopped as he realized we would need to go upstream a ways to be able to get back across to our boulder and the trail beyond. We gauged what we felt was about the right starting point and then took off. Some of us made it to the boulder, and some went a little beyond, but all were able to find an exit and we all met up within minutes.

We ran downstream along the narrow and winding trail. We went for quite long stretches without seeing the river, then it would suddenly pop out here and there with little side trails that led to the edge. We traveled what felt like three miles (probably closer to one) and could not find any trace of Gary.

"He's drowned—you know that, don't you," Vic had said.

We all looked at each other with extreme worry.

"You're crazy," George said, "he'll be fine."

"George, you saw that water and he obviously wasn't a strong swimmer," I added. "We need to go get help."

We started the long hike back to the cabin as fast as we could. It was the longest walk of our lives, and we were all exhausted. We got back to the cabin half expecting, (hoping anyway) that Gary would already be there.

No Gary. No Mrs. Jackson. We all sat down in the cool air-conditioning, gulped down a glass of water, and tried to

The Drowning

come up with our next move. We quickly decided that we would go out and look again. Being young teenagers, we didn't want to get ourselves in trouble unnecessarily, and George still felt Gary had to be OK. We waited another half an hour in the cool. I know—it really seems stupid now.

Hitting the trails again, we walked and walked until darkness was beginning to threaten. It wasn't just the darkness of the night that was coming. We had all grown very quiet as we became convinced that Gary was gone.

We headed back to the cabin because we hadn't brought a flashlight. It was a long trudge of despair. As we crossed a junction in the trail, we heard a howl.

"Wait!" George whispered, "What was that?"

We waited in nervous anticipation. Was that a person or some animal? Nothing but silence followed.

"Gaaarrrrryyyyyy!" George yelled as I jumped out of my skin.

"Whhheeerrrreee aaarrreee yyyouuuu!" came the best sound we ever heard. It was him!

We joined up on the trail and gathered around our fallen friend. He told us how he had struggled in the water. He had slammed against rocks and his arms had become extremely heavy as he tired. He told us how he had felt he was going to die a number of times before he had managed to get out of the water about a mile downstream and had been lost ever since.

"I was lucky," he said to finish his story.

We made our way back to the cabin and rested, took showers, and ate a lot of junk food. Only about three hours later the foreboding possibility of a lost friend was long forgotten, and we embarked on our naked run through the neighboring campground.

Sunday came to Merrimac State Park, and it was time for us to go home. We left the cabin, and Mrs. Jackson promised we would stop at the public beach area in the park for a couple of hours. It was extremely hot and we were glad for the opportunity to take one more swim.

The water here was still fairly swift, but only about knee deep. We all floated, talked, and harassed each other some more. After a time, Mickey, George, and I had floated away from the group. We floated on our backs for a couple minutes in some attempt to see who could do it the longest.

"George! Help me! It's over my head!" Mickey yelled out.

I rolled over and saw the river had taken us quite far downstream remarkably fast. I tried to stand and gulped water as I thought it was over my head as well. I saw George standing as I floated past, so I forced my feet down and they held on some jagged rocks. The water seemed quicker here, and I struggled to hold position in the now chest deep water.

Mickey was now hanging on George's back and George took a couple of steps. "C'mon," he said to me, "it's not that bad."

I felt like if I raised my foot I would fall. I looked around and the water was swirling all around me. I was now scared, because I realized this water was not safe. I could feel the river swirling all around me, relentlessly pushing me back.

"George...wait...I can't move," I said.

George looked at me and said more harshly than he looked, "Stroud, quit being such a wuss and c'mon." He turned around and took another step.

He was out of reach, so I couldn't wait any longer. I took a step, then another. "George," I half pleaded, "hold up. Let's grab arms and help support each other."

The Drowning

George looked at me, and then he turned and looked how far we had to go. I could tell he was getting a little worried as well. I had heard of dangerous currents, but never really believed in them. I was a strong swimmer, and I was indestructible.

I had to go a couple steps to be within reach of George. Just as I was contemplating lifting my foot, I felt something I never had before and never want to again. It felt as if something had grabbed my legs below the knees. The undertow sucked me down harder than I would have ever thought possible. Everything was a swirling mass of anarchy. I was completely helpless. My body twisted, and my knee hit a rock on the bottom hard. I still remember my desperate thought as clear as day, *Oh God, I'm gonna die, help me!*

It seemed as if I had been under for at least thirty seconds, but it had to have been just a couple. Surely, I was a hundred yards or more from George by now. I hadn't hit any more rocks though. Wait, was I moving at all? Yes, I'm moving upstream! Just then I broke the surface and gasped for air. George, our future hero fullback, had Mickey on his back and my wrist firmly in his hand. We worked together to get upstream. After only about fifty yards, the water got a little shallower and then it became much easier.

"George, how did you possibly grab me? You were out of reach. I thought I was gone downstream. That current had me tight, and it wasn't going to let me do anything."

"I dunno. I turned and barely saw you go under. Your arm was outstretched and I just jumped toward it without thinking. It went under, and my hand dove into the water, and somehow locked onto your wrist. I yanked hard and it brought my feet back to the ground. It was so fast..." he trailed off and just shook his head.

I was alive after the only time in my life I thought I was as good as dead. It happened in the blink of an eye, and I still don't know how George rescued Mickey and me in that current. He was strong, and I know he probably would have made it up and out of the river on his own. As far as the jumping back, grabbing me on his only shot, and gaining strong enough footing to pull me out of that undertow—*lucky!*

Miracle Two

Kathy to the Rescue

Remember not the sins of my youth and my rebellious ways; according to your love remember me, for you are good, O LORD.

—Psalm 25:7

I was raised in a suburb of St. Louis, Missouri, in a solid middle class family. From as long as I can remember, the same group of boys lived in the neighborhood and we grew into our teens together. We were somewhat of a gang—hard on each other, but nobody else better take on one of us.

As we grew older we began to get ourselves into bigger and bigger trouble. I should really say potential trouble, because we never really got caught. My first experience with "the dark side" was when I discovered that a certain type of play money that was sold at a small store on one side of the neighborhood would actually fool the dollar change machine at the laundromat on the other side of the neighborhood. We went on a few different days and got about ten bucks each time. Of course, ten bucks then went a lot farther than ten bucks today. Well, I finally did get caught and was grounded for awhile, but I had learned that sometimes you can have a lot of fun being bad.

While most of the stuff we did can be written off as the stupidity of youth, things slowly progressed with each passing year. The older we got the deeper "potential" trouble we got into. Drugs and alcohol were everywhere, and it seemed to fit in very comfortably with the boredom/excitement roller coaster of teenage years in St. Louis.

I was skinny, had bad acne, and was somewhat shy around people I didn't know very well. Therefore, you can imagine that I wasn't a big hit with the girls. There were a few dates, and a couple of girls that wanted us to become a couple. Unfortunately, those girls didn't meet with my friends' approval as they weren't cool enough, or pretty enough, or were just too tall. Really, none of those girls attracted me either and what my friends did was only keeping me from using them further.

There were girls that I fell deeply in love with as well. They could have asked me to do about anything for them, and I would have done it like a well-trained puppy. The only trouble was that these girls weren't interested. Some hardly knew I even existed. Some wanted to be friends and would talk with me for long periods of time, but they were definitely not interested in anything else. Of course, these girls always gained steady boyfriends and I was pushed aside.

So even among my friends, I know now, I had a low self-esteem. I always felt they were stronger, or braver, or cooler than I was. Acne was the problem and I could do nothing about it. It made me self-conscious, it kept the girls away, it made me shy. This low self-esteem made me always want to do things that made my friends talk about me in a positive way. I was generally willing to do anything with them.

My family took a trip to visit my mother's family in Moncks Corner, South Carolina, during the summer between my tenth and eleventh grade. We made this trip every couple years and I always loved it. It was the country, so much different than my home. We fished, we talked, and we harassed the cows instead of stealing, fighting someone, or vandalizing something. We got into some "potential trouble" there as well, but it was nowhere near what was going on back home.

I awoke enveloped in the soft comfort of my Ma-ma's (what we called our grandmother) feather bed and huge feather pillows. I loved that bed. My entire body just sank in and I could sleep no matter what was going on around me. The problem was—Ma-ma wouldn't let me.

"Kevin!...Kevin!" she called from outside the bedroom door.

"Ma'am," I answered. I only answered this way in South Carolina. People didn't talk that way in Missouri—just one of the many little differences that made this part of the world a magical place for me.

"It's eight-thirty, are you going to sleep the entire day away? Get out of that bed and come get some breakfast," she snapped through the door.

"Yes, Ma'am," I answered, immediately wide awake. Ma-ma's cooking was another thing I loved dearly.

I began eating some of the best eggs, bacon, and toast on the planet. I guess it was Ma-ma's chicken farm with the fresh eggs, but that really doesn't explain everything. Moncks Corner and Ma-ma's farm were parts of a glorious new world where everything was different—better. The grass and morning dew smelled different. The dirt roads, electric fences, cattle, and open space made it seem like I had stepped into a new world. Moncks Corner was a world full of opportunity, where I seemed to have a higher self-esteem, more confidence, and my troubles were left behind in St. Louis. This city boy was cool to these country folks.

"Yvonne called this morning and wants you to go with them to Lion's Beach this morning about ten," Ma-ma informed me while I was busy shoving in my breakfast.

"Great!" I said with genuine excitement. Lion's beach, on the shores of the large Lake Moultrie, was always one of our favorite places to go, and I hadn't seen Yvonne, my cousin, for a couple of years.

When the time arrived, I jumped into my parent's car and drove the quarter mile to Yvonne's—she lived next door. I knocked on the door and the door flung open to reveal a beaming Yvonne who quickly grabbed me and wrapped her arms around my neck. Yvonne was probably the prettiest girl to have ever thrown her arms around my neck at that point, and I smiled inwardly as I thought, *Kevin, now watch it, she is your cousin.*

As we walked into the house I did a little bit of a double-take at the pretty girl smiling from the den sofa. Aunt Iris came in and gave me a big hug as we said our hellos.

"Kevin," Yvonne called with that slow southern drawl that everyone had but me, "I want you to meet Kathy. She's been my best friend for years and it's her fifteenth birthday today."

"Hello, Kathy, and happy birthday," I said.

"Hey," she replied.

That first exchange was pretty short. Kathy and I were both pretty shy and if it hadn't been for the fact that we were both comfortable around my cousin, it would have probably ended there.

Kathy to the Rescue

We arrived at Lion's Beach and quickly headed off to the water. We just hung out for awhile in a little over waist deep water for me—chest deep for both girls. Yvonne and Kathy had whispered to each other a couple of times and would never let me in on what they were talking about. They did it again, and again, and I was beginning to get a little self-conscious about the whispering and giggling.

"So…, Kevin…," Yvonne began, but paused as I looked at her. Her eyes took a quick look at Kathy as she began to open her mouth and then blurted, "So what do you think of Kathy?"

Kathy let out a little scream and struggled to grab hold of Yvonne. Yvonne was making a hasty getaway. Suddenly feeling much better about all the whispers, I dove under the water. Swimming slowly, I swam to within a foot or so of Yvonne and Kathy's legs. I stayed pretty motionless and held my breath for about as long as I could. Being a strong swimmer and a member of a local swim team the year before, I could hold my breath quite awhile. You can only see a couple feet below the surface in Lake Moultrie, and we had drifted into deeper water. They had no idea where I was.

I smiled as I waited. This girl must like me, and what's even more surprising, she must like how I look, because we could count the number of words we'd said to each other on our hands.

"Kevin? Where are you?!" I heard Yvonne ask.

As I ran out of air, I came up between Yvonne's legs and quickly raised her on my shoulders. She screamed and laughed, and I quickly raised her feet and flung her upside down in the water.

This started a bit of a dunking war and Yvonne and I wrestled for a few minutes. As I was dunking and being dunked, I saw Kathy standing there alone, and I knew I had to get up the nerve now. Yvonne dunked me again and I disappeared.

I swam ever so slowly over to Kathy, as I heard Yvonne calling after me. I admired the girl from under the water as I slowly snuck around behind her. *This pretty girl likes me,* I thought. *Don't screw this up!*

Kathy tensed as I quickly came up between her legs this time and raised her out of the water. She acted totally surprised and squealed as I threw her off my back and upside down into the water. This had the desired effect, and now we were in a three-way battle to drown each other.

As we settled down and began leaving the water, Yvonne said, "So what do you think about Kathy, Kevin?"

This time I was shocked into silence. What could I say that wasn't completely embarrassing? Kathy dunked Yvonne hard, and I ran the rest of the way out of the water and up to the pavilion and the sanctuary of the pinball machines.

After a little while, Yvonne came up by herself and in a much more serious tone, "Well?"

"Well what?" I asked dumbly.

"Kathy wants to know if you like her or not?"

I, still embarrassed, took a moment and answered, "Yeah."

We spent the rest of the day together and Kathy and I actually began to talk a little more. Now, I was ready for Yvonne to let us alone for awhile so I could get to know this girl. Living in St. Louis and only here for a couple of weeks, I was only thinking that Kathy and I could have some fun. Maybe I would be able to go back to St. Louis and tell my friends a heroic tale of my first sexual conquest.

This kind of stupid thinking should have cost me Kathy. The second day and evening I was all hands and mouth. We went out to the Tail Race canal and took a walk. A slow hike to the Highway 52 bridge, then we climbed up underneath

Kathy to the Rescue

it and sat and talked for awhile. I had a goal now, and it wasn't long before I got up the nerve to move in for our first kiss. The rest of that day, we kissed a lot and Kathy fought off my hands a few times.

I took her to the Swamp Fox drive-in theater that night. We didn't really watch a lot of the movie. I had really begun to like this girl, but I was going to have to leave and I still had to achieve my conquest and have my great tale. So I leaned over and kissed her, my hand resting on her leg. I kept kissing as my hand slid up and began trying to undo the button of her jeans. For a second, I thought Kathy was actually letting me. Truth be told, she was in a bit of shock that this boy who she was beginning to like a lot would try such a thing, especially on their first real date. She grabbed my wrist and moved it away from her as she stopped kissing me and said, "No."

That move had taken every ounce of courage I had in me. I had fought myself the whole way to try it. I felt bad about trying it, but I just had to see if I could get my story that would earn temporary admiration from my friends back home. Now I was crushed. I felt badly for trying it with this very pretty girl who had really seemed to like me. What kind of person am I?

We sat there for awhile and pretended to watch the movie and I finally asked, "Do you want to go?"

The answer confirmed my fears. "Yeah," she whispered.

Sleep wasn't easy that night. My thoughts swirled around how I'd blown it with a girl I liked very much and, for once, liked me back. How could I have been so stupid? I had given her a little goodnight kiss when we parted, but I didn't know what to say. I should have apologized, but I didn't.

Somewhere around lunchtime the next day I couldn't take it any longer. Kathy was the only thing that I could think about, and I had to see if I could salvage something of my disaster. I called her and she answered the phone. Caught off guard, my brain stumbled with what to say.

"...Kathy?" I asked, stalling for time to get my thoughts in order.

"Hey," came the reply.

I swallowed and plowed ahead, "Kathy, can we go do something? "

"Yeah," came the simple reply. Kathy wasn't trying to make this any easier on me.

"Okay, I'll pick you up in about an hour."

"Okay. Bye," and she was gone.

Kathy agreeing to meet with me was cause for subdued elation. I could tell by her voice that she wasn't completely happy with me, and I feared a little that she only agreed to go do something so she could tell me to take a hike in person.

Our third day together went wonderfully. We didn't do anything special. We just kind of drove around or sat under trees and talked. My main memory of that third day is the elation I felt that she still liked me and the feeling that came over me as I tried to go to sleep that night. Thoughts of her kept me awake practically all night. Thoughts of a gentle touch, my hand resting on the curve of her hip as we walked, holding hands and talking under a large oak tree. Thoughts of tomorrow and the promise of new treasured feelings it would bring. I was head over heals in love with this girl.

Not only was she the prettiest girl I'd ever dated, but she *really* liked me. She liked me enough to forgive my idiotic actions on our first date and give me another chance. She seemed as thrilled as I that things had worked themselves out and we were getting so comfortable with each other.

When I left South Carolina that summer and returned to St. Louis, I was a different person. I had a girl who was in love with me, and I was in love with her. It was hard to leave her and our eyes watered as we said good-bye.

We spent the next four months writing each other almost every day. Our letters progressed along with our feelings for each other and how much we missed being together. I fell more and more in love with her through the mail and over the phone.

My friends had a mixed review. Some thought it was great and some took it as an opportunity to tell me how much of a *wimp* (I won't use the real word here) I was. Some thought it was just ridiculous to think you could fall in love at that age. Ours was an age to party, experience as many girls as we could, and party some more. "Forget her," they'd say. "Let's go find some trouble."

I became better friends with the ones who thought Kathy and I were a wonderful thing and grew apart from the others. All of them continued to experiment with things that were leading to some serious trouble. I found reasons not to do this or that, or went and hung with this friend so I wouldn't have to do *that* with another. My relationship with Kathy was already working on me. I still went out and drank more than I should or smoked more than I should, but I did not progress further along this road like most of my friends did.

Christmas break from school finally arrived and I flew down to South Carolina for the two weeks. During this time, Kathy and I were only separated because we were forced to be at night. While we had a lot of fun and learned a lot about each other, our upcoming separation again was always weighing us down. We talked about plans of me spending the whole summer there and then Christmas next year. After that, I would graduate high school and move down here and be with her.

After I returned to St. Louis, time stood still. I really was down to only two friends up there now, because all I ever talked about was Kathy, Kathy, and more Kathy. My other friends partied and partied. Most had grades that were either failing or barely passing, and they didn't even care about it. Peer pressure ensured I only made Bs and Cs, because it didn't bode well with any of these *friends* if I did too well.

I sent my young love flowers on Valentines Day. Disappointed when I didn't receive anything from her, I called to make sure she received my gift.

"Hello, Kathy," I said.

"Uh-hmm," came the reply.

"What's the matter?" I asked.

"Nothing," she whispered.

"Did you get the flowers?"

There was only silence on the other end. I was getting really nervous now, something was wrong with her.

"Kathy, tell me what's the matter," I demanded.

Again, only silence. I was getting a little annoyed now, and I only asked the next question to get a response. "Do you still love me, or are you wanting to break up?"

I was shocked when the only answer was more silence. We sat there for probably three minutes, neither of us saying a word. My chest was bursting with nerves. It felt as if my heart was being yanked through my chest. I had learned to not trust anyone because even your best friends would hurt you. Then, believing this was no longer true, I gave my heart over completely to a sweet southern belle whom I loved so, so much.

"Why?" I whispered.

"We're too far apart," came her whisper in return.

"Kathy, we talked about this. I'm coming to stay the whole summer in just three and a half months." Even I could hear the tone of a beggar in my voice.

Silence.

"Do you want to break up?" I forced out of my mouth. My chest was going to burst, and I was going to die right there, I just knew it.

"Yes," she whispered so softly that I could barely hear her.

I hung up the phone and just sat in my basement room completely stunned. At first, I felt nothing. This just couldn't be real. Finally, I had learned there was love out there and the world wasn't such a bad place. Now my world crashed all around me. I kept thinking, *What can I do—there has to be something—what?!*

Suddenly, I broke free. I ran to my bed and cried into my pillow. I felt so betrayed. I felt like there really was no point to living. I felt I was so very weak to cry like this over some girl eight hundred miles away. I should have known better. I should have never put down my guard.

The next four months were probably the most dangerous four months of my life. I became a mean member of what really was a gang (although we never called it that back then). We lived to drink, smoke dope, and try to find women to *party* with. One night, we stole over $500 in soda bottles. At just a five cent return per bottle and two dollars per wooden crate, we had a lot of soda bottles. One of my friends had acquired some bolt cutters and we went around to numerous gas stations and broke in and took all the used bottles they had. One gas station alone had a ten by twelve foot shed completely filled with cases of empty bottles. If someone had confronted us that night, I have little doubt that someone would have assaulted that person and the rest of us would have joined in. We split up the cases between

One Man's Miracles

a couple pickup trucks and a couple cars. We spent the rest of that night driving around town cashing in bottles at many different places.

One day about ten of us walked up to a church and challenged their congregation. Two boys had made a comment about my long hair as I walked past a little earlier. I just mentioned this to a guy who was the leader of our neighborhood gang, and the next thing I know we are all up there with knives, chains, and baseball bats and about to beat two teenage boys. If someone from that church hadn't seen us coming and the entire congregation hadn't spilled out in front of us, either or both of those two boys could easily have been killed. We turned and left when a man told us the police were on their way.

Another time, one of my friends in the car in front of mine hit a stop sign going over a hundred miles per hour, as he tried to make a quick move to shake a cop on his tail. The car flew for a few hundred feet as the landing was much lower than the takeoff. Somehow, everyone survived with only minor injuries.

Someone was always stealing something, fighting someone, or vandalizing property somewhere, and I just didn't care anymore. As long as I was having fun, the rest didn't matter. At the end of May, I was at the house of this same "leader"—he was twenty-three years old and I was seventeen at the time. Another person in his twenties came in and pulled out some needles and asked who was going to shoot up with him. Everyone else in the room said they would like to try it. I was shocked.

I had an uncle who had gotten mixed up with hard drugs when I was only about ten years old. He went to jail for armed robbery of a drugstore. His was the only funeral that I had attended at this point in my life. He had been raped and butchered with a butter knife from the prison chow hall.

I suddenly felt I had to act quickly as if my very life depended on it. It was dark outside and the stereo was blaring as usual. So, as everyone focused on the first person taking a needle in his arm, I quietly snuck out the back door and walked home.

I made up my mind on that walk home. I had to try. I had to get out of this town. I waited up until morning and told my parents I was going to South Carolina to spend the summer there and stay with Ma-ma. If it was the tone in my voice or they just thought it would be good for me as well, I'm not sure, but Mom made the call right there and Ma-ma said it was okay.

I finished my last two weeks of school and just dodged questions about my whereabouts that night, or said I couldn't when asked by others to do something. One friend of mine, Teddy, knew I planned not to return. Being a year older, he was about to leave for a stint in the Army. He knew he had to get out as well.

I drove to South Carolina and arrived at Ma-ma's about seven o'clock in the evening. Somewhere in our conversation that night, Ma-ma said, "I saw Yvonne and Kathy the other day. Kathy asked about you and I told her you were coming." Then, peering over her glasses and the crochet project she was working on, she added, "Kathy seemed pretty happy about that."

I forced down the well up of emotion trying to force its way to the top. There was no way I would let myself believe that it was going to be that easy. Oh, I had no doubt that Kathy was going to be mine; I just figured it was going to take some effort.

The next morning, I pulled into Kathy's driveway and slowly got out of my car. I planned just to knock on the door, say hello, and hopefully talk on the porch for a few minutes. The back door slammed shut and I looked up to see Kathy, even more beautiful than I remembered, running to me with one of the biggest smiles I had ever seen. She jumped and wrapped her arms around my neck and legs around my waist. She kissed me deeply for quite a long time.

I could not believe it. It was as if nothing had ever happened. Kathy was there, she wanted me, and she loved me. We picked up right where we'd left each other over Christmas. The subject of the breakup didn't even come up for a couple weeks. I was afraid if I brought it up she would suddenly remember and run off in horror that she had forgotten such a thing.

When we finally did talk about it, Kathy said she just couldn't believe that any guy could really love her as much as she loved me. She felt we couldn't wait at our age for a couple years to be together and not date with their friends. She felt horrible about it and had thought of calling many, many times.

Late that summer, I called home and told my parents that I wasn't coming home. After a very difficult conversation and me actually resorting to confessing things I never thought I would actually tell my parents, they relented. They asked my uncle to act as legal guardian for the next year. I finished my last year of high school in Moncks Corner and married Kathy two weeks before her seventeenth birthday. It seemed as if no one really gave us a shot at lasting. I joined the Air Force and we began our life together. We've been married twenty-seven years and counting.

I was completely lost in St. Louis. It seems that a couple of my friends spent some time in jail. Another was killed in some sort of drug incident. I generally lost track and have only talked with a couple of them just once since I left St. Louis. I have lived around the world, earned a Master's

Degree in Business, and was commissioned as an officer. I have succeeded in life far more than I thought I would in the early years of high school. Meeting Kathy gave me hope in a time when I really didn't have any. She accepted me with all my faults and forgave me when I tried to screw it up. Falling in love, and then deepening it over Christmas, convinced me I had to do better in my life. The breakup and subsequent loss of hope caused me to hit rock bottom and showed me where my life could very easily go—most likely, if not for the lesson of my uncle's horrible death, where my life may very well have still ended up. Then finally, the ease with which I was able to escape that life by Kathy running to jump back into my arms. I sure was *lucky*.

Miracle Three
The Propeller

> The LORD will keep you from all harm—he will watch over your life; ....
>
> —Psalm 121:7

I kissed Kathy gently on the cheek and left for my second real day on the job. While I had been in Germany for a couple weeks inprocessing, getting a driver's license, and training on the OV-10 Bronco, Kathy had just arrived. We were stationed at Sembach Air Base in Germany, and we lived about forty minutes from the base in a small town called Diemerstein (I think) just outside of Frankenstein (that's one place I'll never forget). It was about 5:45 A.M. and still dark as I negotiated the curves of the small, dark country roads in a little Citroen that I had purchased as soon as I arrived.

During the drive I thought about how nice my life was turning out. I had a beautiful wife, a job I liked, and we were seeing the world. I loved what I saw of Germany so far, and couldn't wait until we could go explore. I was relieved that Gary and Elke had come to our house that first night of Kathy's arrival. She and Elke hit it off, and that would ease her transition to a different way of life than we had ever experienced. Gary was another airman, and I roomed with him the first couple weeks when I arrived. Elke was a German girl he had been dating for a couple of years. We became very close to Gary and Elke over the course of the four and a half years we were in Germany. They would turn out to be the best friends we would ever have.

It took me a little longer to get to work than I'd planned. The roads had been a little icy, and as I rolled down the window to show the gate guard my ID, I felt a chill course through me. I hurried to the little building where they took roll call in the morning. I made it just in time and saw one of the avionics technicians light a bag of Lipton tea on fire and then blow it out and let it smolder in the ashtray. A bunch of guys were struggling to keep in the laughter as our maintenance officer, who really looked kind of like a weasel with glasses and never did earn anyone's respect, began to speak.

Suddenly, I smelled it. That burning tea smelled almost exactly like marijuana. A laugh involuntarily burst from my mouth and I quickly looked down as I saw the lieutenant's eyes move toward me. Luckily, just as he was about to let me have it he raised his nose and sniffed. He turned sharply to his right and sniffed again.

"Who's been smoking marijuana?!" he yelled.

Everyone looked around, mumbling things like, "I dunno, do you know? I smell it too."

"Squadron, 'tench hut!" barked our first sergeant after about thirty seconds of humorous chaos. The first sergeant had everyone's respect. Not just because we had to give it to him, but because he deserved it.

Everyone came to attention immediately and you could have heard a pin drop. Well, we could all hear the lieutenant sniffing as he followed his nose. He stuck his nose to one

The Propeller

airman's chest, then satisfied the odor wasn't coming from him, he sniffed and moved again.

The little snickers started, and then the almost painful grunts and watery eyes began as the lieutenant neared the ashtray. He saw the smoke and yelled, "What is going on, someone's smoking this stuff in here?!"

The first sergeant himself couldn't help but smile as he realized what it was, and when Senior Airman Phelps said, "Sorry, sir. I didn't have any water so I decided to try smoking my morning tea. It didn't taste so great, but I got my caffeine fix."

The entire place exploded in laughter. The first sergeant just shook his head and returned to his desk. The lieutenant gave a little nervous laugh and told Tiny (the biggest master sergeant I'd ever seen) to get us out to work. Jokes are a part of military life. Those who can take it as well as shell it out always succeeded as members of the team. There was a line, however, that folks had to know not to cross.

New guys usually got sent out for a "bucket of prop wash" or a "piece of flight line." Neither of these things are items you can acquire, of course. Prop wash is the turbulent air behind a propeller that is thrusting a plane forward. Flight line is the ramp area where aircraft are readied for flight. Everyone at the base, except for the poor newbie, knew the joke, and when an airman came and asked, they would be sent somewhere else on the base to find it. As new guys didn't want to fail their first real task, they were often gone for hours on this wild goose chase. These types of jokes were okay, or at least tolerated, but any horseplay that could hurt someone was generally dealt with swiftly.

Since this was my second base, I was beyond such embarrassing activities. I was anxious to get to work and become a valuable member of my new team.

One Man's Miracles

We drove up and got our tools, and then Tiny drove us out to the various aircraft. He'd pull up to one and yell out what had to be done and who, if anyone, was to jump out along with the crew chief to assist in the work.

"Stroud, you signed off as a fire guard yet?" Tiny boomed out.

"Yeah, got it done yesterday," I replied.

"Good, get out there and do it. Jones, this aircraft needs an engine run operational check," Tiny ordered.

Just then, everyone caught a whiff of the disgusting smell. Tiny opened the door of the truck and yelled, "Damn it! Who had something die in 'em last night?"

The back doors flung open and everyone cleared the truck except Cox. He sat there laughing and saying, "Yeah! I'm proud of that one. I cleared the whole truck!"

He thoroughly enjoyed taunting everyone as they climbed back into the truck, mumbling things about Cox's upbringing and his wife's cooking. As the truck pulled away, I heard Cox yell out, "Ow!" and the truck erupted in laughter again.

Jones did a quick walk around as I removed all the safety plugs from the engine inlets and exhaust of the OV-10. Jones jumped up in the cockpit and said something about not freezing, and then laughed at me as he shut the canopy. As soon as he got the engines started, he would have heat.

Jones was kind of a sloppy airman who came off with an attitude of superiority to anyone who wasn't at least a staff sergeant like himself. Although still too new to the squadron to know for sure, my first impression wasn't good, and I didn't think he was particularly well liked.

I stood by the exhaust of the portable light-all that kept the aircraft lit in the darkness. The exhaust helped a good deal with the bitter cold, as there was nothing out on the flight line to break the wind.

The Propeller

I looked at this strange-looking airplane. The OV-10 Bronco was a two-engine, turbo-propeller plane. It had a center section where the pilot sat and a small cargo area behind him. Off each wing ran a tail boom that turned into two rudders and joined up with the stabilizer at the top. It looked like no other plane I had seen or have seen since. It was used in Vietnam to fly around and mark where the F-4 Phantoms were to do the heavy work of war.

Jones raised one finger and then spun it like it was winding something up. This was my cue that he wanted to start the number one engine. I checked that all was clear, gave him the thumbs up, and the propeller began to turn. It slowly built up speed until it smoothly sang out against the morning peacefulness. I watched while leaning against a huge fire extinguisher just in case something went wrong and there was a fire.

With number one running freely now, I moved around to the number two side and leaned onto that fire extinguisher. Jones raised two fingers and spun them up. I checked that the number two engine was clear and gave him the thumbs up again. The engine slowly chugged up speed. For a second, I didn't think it was going to start, but then it caught and ran up to its full idle speed.

Both engines were very loud and we wore hearing protection under headsets where we could talk to each other. I heard him call for clearance to run and mumble a couple of items on his checklist, but Jones and I really hadn't said anything to each other.

Suddenly, I heard Jones yell, "Oh, crap!" and I looked up to see him looking over his left shoulder. Smoke was billowing out of the number one engine. I had to act. I had to get to the number one fire extinguisher and get the fire out. If the fire spread, Jones could be trapped or, more likely, we could lose an aircraft.

I shot around the back of the plane. I held my head low as I came around to the number one side. I looked at the ground and ran to the front. At idle, the propellers are angled to not provide any thrust, so there is no air being pushed behind the aircraft and it is safe to move behind it.

Suddenly, I heard a voice in my head yell, "Prop!" I stopped cold, frozen in place as I felt the vibration of the spinning propeller. I slowly raised my eyes and was shocked to see the propeller spinning mere inches from my head. They paint stripes on the top of the propellers so you can see them while they are spinning, but I didn't need that paint. I was directly in back of a blade that would dice me up and spit me out like I wasn't even there. I was afraid to move. I was afraid that if I did, some part of my body would shift into the blade path.

Then, I remembered the fire again and forced myself to back away from the prop. I ran to the fire extinguisher, grabbed the hose, and charged the handle. I looked to the engine and there was no fire, no smoke. I looked back to Jones and he was sitting in the cockpit laughing and pointing at me. He showed me one finger and animatedly lowered it to an unseen switch. Smoke billowed from the number one tailpipe. It was a smoke generator and was used along with phosphorous rockets to mark targets.

I staggered. I was dizzy—probably because I just then started to breathe and was hyperventilating. I stumbled to the edge of the run pad and sat down on the curb. I was shivering uncontrollably, but was suddenly very hot. I wrapped my arms around my knees and laid my head upon them. I felt sick. My whole body kept shaking, I couldn't stop.

I heard the truck speed up to the aircraft. I heard Tiny jump out and yell and scream for Jones to shut down the *expletive* engines. I heard the engines shut off and I forced

The Propeller

myself to my feet. I was still shaking but I was going to kill Jones. I looked toward the cockpit and Tiny was already standing on the step and he had Jones by the collar. I saw him literally yank Jones out of that aircraft and throw him into the truck.

A launch truck pulled up and asked me if I needed a ride. I nodded and climbed in. My body still shivered, because I knew I had come within a literal inch of my life. I thought of Kathy and the unborn children we wanted to have. I thought of my parents and them receiving such crushing news. I thought of my head exploding like some kind of overripe watermelon thrown onto the ground.

I did not see Jones again for a month. I heard he was being given every kind of additional duty the first sergeant could think of, and I was satisfied with that.

I can still see that prop when I think about it. I can still feel the vibration throbbing against my head. I can still hear that voice yelling out just before impact. That sure was *lucky*.

Miracle Four

Births

Sons are a heritage from the LORD, children a reward from him.

—Psalm 127:3

I cannot imagine anyone who has ever witnessed birth denying that it is a miracle in itself. Science may be able to explain it and recognize what is happening, but they'll never know all the *hows*.

Kathy and I had been trying to have a baby for over three years. We both went for various tests and it boiled down to me having a low sperm count. Everyone gave me their suggestions, like eating oysters, taking vitamins, et cetera. Nothing worked and the disappointment we felt when each menstruation came was tough.

I left for a six-week temporary duty to Zarogosa Air Base, Spain, in late September 1983. I was a dedicated crew chief on an OV-10, and where my plane went I went. This was my first trip to Spain and I was excited to explore a new country during my time off. We didn't really get much time off on these trips. We generally worked twelve hour shifts, six days per week, but we didn't sleep much either.

One Man's Miracles

On one of my few days off, a friend and I decided to hit the shopping area of Zaragosa. There were not many of us who went on trips like this because, being young and in the military, many had to rest up for yet another night of drinking. The Zaragosa shops were located in narrow streets called "the tubes." They were small shops with specialized merchandise. I really didn't see anything to buy until we passed a store with what I thought were the most beautiful baby blankets I'd ever seen. I went in and felt how soft they were and dreamed what it would be like to have a baby wrapped inside. After three years, and practically giving up on ever having a baby, I was moved to buy two of these blankets.

About a week after I returned home, Kathy informed me she was ten days late for her period. We ran out and bought a home pregnancy test kit. We had done this once before and were sorely disappointed so we tried not to be optimistic. We watched the indicator closely for a few seconds, and then decided to put it down and walk away. After the required time, Kathy and I walked in together and saw the results. We began jumping and hollering and hugging and dreaming. Kathy was pregnant at last.

Jennifer was born late at night on May 24, 1984, at Landstuhl Army Hospital in Germany. Kathy's water had broken the night before and we had spent twenty-four hours waiting—twelve of which Kathy was in labor.

I watched in complete awe as my baby's head came into view. It was misshapen at first and about three different shades of red and green. Videos had prepared me for this, so I wasn't worried at all. Misshapen or not, it was the most beautiful head I had ever seen.

Kathy was doing wonderfully and had only yelled at me a couple of times. She was tense and in pain and I, in not one of my brightest moments, thought I'd try to lighten the mood. I looked down at her and said excitedly, "Oh, Honey, it's a Yoda!"

Kathy scowled at me in such a way that I knew I had made a terrible mistake. Her sense of humor was gone. Luckily for me, she was told to push. Still, she squeezed my hand much harder than any other time that night.

I thought I had wanted a boy, but I was thrilled it was a baby girl. She was healthy and beautiful. The first time I held Jennifer my heart completely melted, and I knew she would learn that she had her daddy wrapped around her finger at a pretty young age.

June 24, 1988. We were now stationed at Eglin Air Force Base, Fort Walton Beach, Florida, and Kathy was about to give birth again. Kathy had a little bit rougher pregnancy this time. She had suffered sun poisoning at one point, ran high sugar for most of it, and had swelled much more than with Jennifer. This birth, however, seemed like it was going quickly, for almost as soon as we had arrived the nurse said, "She's dilated, let's get her into the delivery room."

We had been told that it looked like this was a boy, and I was excited. The doctor came in and she said it wouldn't be long now as she finished prepping the room.

"Okay, Kathy," the doctor said, "I want you to push for me."

Kathy began pushing. She pushed with each contraction and quickly looked as if her head was going to burst. I debated about making a comment about a giant pimple, but being one who generally learns from his mistakes, I kept my mouth shut.

"Kathy, listen to me, I really need you to give it a hard push this time," said the doctor. I looked at the doctor and everything seemed fine. I didn't remember Kathy taking so long last time, once the delivery actually began.

Finally, the head emerged and the doctor said, "This is a big baby!" I swelled with pride that my future running back was already getting compliments on his size.

Kathy began pushing and pushing. The doctor urged her on. The baby didn't want to come out any further. The doctor's urging became more pitched. On the next push, it looked to me as if the doctor's feet left the floor as she pushed down on my baby's head. Still, the baby didn't move.

"Kathy, you are going to have to give it everything you have, now push!" the doctor urged. Then, after a long hard push, Kathy's eyes rolled back into her head and her body began to shake. I looked at the doctor and saw fear in her face.

My eyes began to water. My body was momentarily frozen. Something had gone horribly wrong. I heard the doctor say in what seemed like slow motion, "We should have done a C-section!"

She had to be killing the baby the way she was pulling and twisting on its head. I could tell that Kathy didn't have much left in her. The doctor yelled, "We have to get this baby out, *now!*"

The room began to slowly spin and I could hear my heart pumping loudly in my head. I heard a loud audible gasp, then realized it was from me. Oh, God, help them. This can't be happening. The nurses ran to both sides of Kathy and forcibly pushed me out of the way. They grabbed her ankles and began pulling her legs over her head. I spun around and saw the doors and momentarily headed that way, as if I could escape this nightmare. What was I doing?! I couldn't escape this by leaving my wife and baby! I turned back and heard a loud pop! The baby was out. The doctor didn't hand the baby off, but took it to a table. I noticed her begin working in a controlled, deliberate, but seemingly frantic, manner. She still looked nervous.

Kathy was shaking terribly. Her lips were blue and I heard a nurse whisper something about shock. Kathy tried to say something, but I couldn't make it out.

I rubbed her head and it felt cold and clammy, "Quiet, Honey. It's okay, rest."

She wasn't about to rest until I understood her. She strained to get out a whisper, "Is the baby OK?"

"Yes," I lied, and Kathy's eyes closed.

It seemed like an eternity had gone by and there was no sound from the baby—it was probably more like forty-five seconds. Suddenly, there was a booming scream that filled the room. He had been building that one up—what a set of lungs!

The doctor finally turned and said, "Here is your beautiful baby girl!"

"Our what...?" I asked. "They said it was a boy."

"Well, they were wrong," she smiled.

After a couple of seconds of silence, the doctor broke my awe of the beautiful, *fat* baby girl with, "I'm sorry but you will have to go to the waiting room now. Someone will come to get you."

She called to Kathy and held the baby next to her. I looked inward to find the disappointment I surely must be feeling that I wasn't getting a son, but it wasn't there. I was thrilled to have another beautiful, *big* baby girl. Kathy's eyes flinched but did not open.

"Is she going to be okay?" I asked, as the doctor gave me a *please leave now* look.

"I think she'll be fine. We just need to treat her for some mild shock—she really had to work for this one," the doctor said.

I went to the waiting room and found Kathy's mother, Katherine, and our nephew, Kevin. Katherine looked up at me with anxious eyes and asked, "Well?"

"It's a *big* girl. I don't know the weight yet."

Katherine clapped her hands and laughed, "Another girl, ohhh boy!"

Then the question I myself was agonizing over, "Are they OK?" she asked.

I answered, "Yeah..., well..., yeah, I think." I saw her eyes widen in fear and I quickly added, "They asked me to leave, but said they should be OK. The baby was just so big, and Kathy's so small." I tried to sound calm, but my voice cracked a couple of times and betrayed my worry.

Katherine sensed this and just said, "Good, they'll be just fine."

I then began pacing the waiting room, the hallway, the waiting room, and then the hallway again. What could be taking so long? I now knew the agony fathers used to routinely have to endure by sitting in the waiting rooms instead of being allowed to be a part of the delivery.

Finally, the nurse came into the waiting room and said that I could go into Kathy's room. I entered her room just before Kathy was rolled in. She was shaking uncontrollably, but the nurse said she would be fine. Then they brought in our beautiful Stephanie.

"Here she is," the nurse crooned, "yes, she is!" She put the baby against her mother and Kathy tried to hold her, but didn't have the strength to do it alone.

"You have to be careful of the broken shoulder," the nurse said.

"What?" Kathy and I asked simultaneously.

"Oh, you didn't know? Well, this little girl was just too big to come through that birth canal. Something had to give, and it was her shoulder. It will be okay, you will just have to be very gentle with it for a few weeks."

I looked at my daughter with wonder. That's what I call fighting your way into the world. She looked at me, and my heart melted again. Now I had two girls and I was so, so happy. I used to think I had to have one son, but I no longer felt that way. Jennifer was a big baby, but at ten pounds thirteen and one half ounces, Stephanie was bigger. I had thought I might lose Kathy. This was going to be our last baby, and I was thrilled to have the perfect family.

I still don't know how that doctor didn't break the baby's neck the way she was yanking and twisting on the head. I don't know for sure, but by the look on her face and the way she ran away with the baby when first delivered, I think maybe she was a little surprised only a shoulder was broken. I felt as if I'd been on a roller coaster. From the happy expectation, to the horror of possibly losing my wife and child, to complete and utter relief, and finally elation and pride for my new girl.

We sure were *lucky*.

Miracle Five
Jennifer's Dive

And he took the children in his arms, put his hands on them and blessed them.

—Mark 10:16

Our little Jennifer had been such a blessing in our life. As an infant, she only woke up during the first night and then slept through the entire night from then on. We could not get enough of this little helpless child looking up at us with such wonder and delight (I know, they say it's gas bubbles). It's truly amazing how something so tiny can bring so much joy to life and at times, so much worry.

A week after we brought her home, I picked Jennifer up and was shocked by the way she just hung limp in my arms like a rag doll. I could feel the fever and her breathing, but Kathy almost passed out when she saw our baby hanging in my arms with eyes wide open.

"Is she de…?" Kathy began but put her hand over her mouth to stop the question's completion.

"No," I assured her that the baby was breathing, but burning up.

We rushed Jennifer to the hospital, and after some tests they concluded it was a mild seizure brought on by fever. We watched from the hallway as five nurses went into the room to hold an infant down for a spinal tap. I'll never forget the horrible scream that came from my little girl, nor how I felt completely helpless. It was a scare we hoped we'd never have again.

Months later, I sat in the living room watching television on a lazy Sunday afternoon. Kathy, Jennifer, and I now lived in Vogelweh military housing on the edge of Kaiserslautern, Germany. Kathy and I should have enjoyed living in our small German village away from the "Little America" of Kaiserslautern. Unfortunately, it turned out the hot water and heat came from a computerized wood burning stove. This system worked great, except when the landlord drank too much and forgot to put wood in it, which was nearly always. We had spent much of the winter huddled in the small kitchen in an otherwise huge apartment, with all four gas burners on high. As soon as we were offered military housing, we ran to the warmth it offered.

We were on the third floor, and it offered adequate space and was comfortable. Elke and Gary had recently moved into the housing development nearby and were to come over later that night for dinner and to watch a football game. Elke had left a little while ago, when she and Kathy put Jennifer down for a nap. Jennifer and Elke often acted like best friends, and just before Jennifer's nap they both had fun pointing at me and repeating one of Jennifer's first words, "Geek!"

Jennifer was now crawling all over the place and pulling herself into standing positions. This meant absolutely everything had to be more than four feet off the ground or it was going to be broken, in Jennifer's mouth, or both.

Jennifer's Dive

Kathy was in the kitchen getting things ready to cook for dinner that evening, and Jennifer had been asleep for about half an hour. I got up and went in there and opened the refrigerator for something, then decided I didn't want anything. Kathy was saying something to me, but I didn't hear her.

Everything moved very slowly from that moment, and my vision tunneled to Jennifer, who had just reached the top of her crib railing. I started to move, but my legs felt as if they were made of cement. The hallway to her room suddenly seemed unbelievably long. Jennifer pitched forward and began a head first dive to the hard tiled floor below. I wasn't going to make it, and she was going to crack her skull open.

I dove down the hallway and into her room and stretched out like a football player trying to break up a play. My hand scooted just off the floor and my fingers just reached the crown of her head. My momentum carried me forward and pushed her as she fell. Her head fell into my palm, then her body flipped onto my arm. She ended up with a very soft landing, and she laughed out loud as she looked at me.

Kathy came running into the room and scooped Jennifer into her protective arms, and Jennifer pointed at me as they walked away. "Geek!" she said, and squealed with laughter.

I laid there on the floor for a few minutes, still not sure how I had made it. If I had not come into the kitchen, or looked her way at that precise moment, or even if I had grabbed something out of the refrigerator like I had gotten up to do, Jennifer would surely have at least been making a trip to the emergency room by ambulance. It would probably have been much worse. That was so very *lucky*.

Miracle Six
Kathy to the Rescue Part II

> In him we have redemption through his blood, the forgiveness of sins, in accordance with the riches of God's grace.
>
> —Ephesians 1:7

I guess it's a lucky man who can look back on his life and not have any big regrets. I should be one of those men. I have been successful at work that I've always liked, and I have been blessed with a wonderful family, including two wonderful daughters of whom I am so very proud. But I'm not one of those lucky men. I have one regret that will pain me for the rest of my life. God has forgiven me, and Kathy has forgiven me, but I will never forgive myself.

It was 1990 and we were stationed at Eglin Air Force Base in Florida. We had bought our first house when we arrived in 1987. It was a small three-bedroom patio home and was only about 1,050 square feet, but we were proud to have achieved this part of the American dream. Jennifer was in school now, and Stephanie had turned two years old. We were in debt, a lot of debt compared to my income. Kathy worked full time in the base dining facility from about 4:30 A.M. to 1:00 P.M. every day of the week. On top of that, she had to come home and take care of a two-year old, still be up to greet Jennifer when she got off the school bus, and then supervise them until I got home.

I hardly ever really got home, however. I was the H-60 helicopter and C-130 aircraft instrumentation, auto-pilot, and inertial navigation supervisor in a Special Operations squadron. I had about fifteen people working for me, and this was my first real leadership role. We were a very active unit and took part in numerous world events. We searched for a senator in Africa, were major players in Panama and in bringing Manuel Noriega to justice, trained with Army Special Operations, and now we were gearing up for Desert Storm.

I was also working on my Bachelor's degree, which I had worked on whenever my job permitted, and it had taken me ten years. I was going to finish in December. My last year of school consisted of a total of forty-three semester hours of credit. While the Air Force allowed me to go full-time to college for two semesters, I still had work and school for the majority of the year, because base colleges usually operate on shorter terms so they can get in five academic terms in a calendar year. I was driven to finally get this done, because I had dreamed of becoming an officer since I first went into the Air Force. The main reason for this dream was I felt a need to be able to provide my family with more money, because despite what everybody always says, I believed money could make us happier. The bottom line to this situation was that I was either at work, at school, or thinking about work, or doing homework. You had to achieve very good grades and have outstanding performance reports to have a shot at getting into Officer Training School.

It was hard times for both of us. But now when I think of it, I realize that Kathy didn't get very much sleep that year. Our relationship was strained for the first time in ten years of marriage. We hardly saw each other, and when we did we were just too tired to offer the other any of ourselves. I kept telling myself, and Kathy, we just have to get through this year and I'll become an officer, and then we'll have our reward.

I applied for Officer Training School when I was within fifteen semester hours of completing my degree. I had glowing recommendations and was on track to graduate Magna Cum Laude. I was confident, and my commanding officers told me that I was a shoe-in. This made the crash that much harder when the answer came.

They don't tell you if you're not accepted. They just publish the names of the nominees. I slowly looked up and down the list and could not believe that I couldn't find my name. We had just finished some rounds of "Reduction in Forces," and they were not taking in many officers. The message said that only one of every ten applicants was selected. Kathy and I had worked so hard, for so long, and it was for nothing. Yeah, I would have a degree, but there was no way I was going to get out of the Air Force until I had twenty years of service. At that moment, I could not see what the degree was going to get me.

I still had to work and finish school because it was mandated since I had gone full-time for two terms. I was broken. I was a failure. I was doomed to never have enough money to do anything with my girls.

In the coming weeks I entered a dark depression. I could see no way out of this hole. I had given it my best shot, and now I had to accept that my life sucked. Kathy and I had grown apart. What did we have in common? I didn't even know her! She never wanted to spend time with me. These were the thoughts going through my head.

One time I cried out to her, but not really in any way she could recognize. I grabbed her as she walked by me sitting on the couch and dragged her on top of me. She was straddling me and I wanted to hug her.

"Kevin...I'm exhausted now, I've got to go to bed," she said.

I was heartbroken by that response. I asked her, "Kathy, do you still love me?"

"Yes. Now let me go."

"Why do you say that? Why do you love me? Do we have anything in common?" I was beginning to get angry.

She hugged me and gave me a gentle kiss.

I pleaded, "Kathy, I really need to know that you still love me right now."

She looked at me with very tired eyes and said, "I love you, Kevin. Can't we talk about this later? I have to get up in about four hours."

"Yeah," I said as I let her up.

I remember very distinctly the feel of cold steel in my mouth as I sat on the edge of the bed with the shotgun loaded. I stood it on the floor and bent over the barrel. Then my hand began sliding down the barrel to the trigger. I had to admit that I was trapped and my family would just be better off without me. I kept imagining the mess I was going to make and Kathy, or one of the girls, finding me. My hand hovered over the trigger. *One..., two..., th...Damn! I don't even have the courage to do this!* I stood up, unloaded the gun, and put it back into the closet.

The buildup in Iraq had been going on for some time, and within days of my inability to end my life, we were told we needed to be ready to deploy at any time. We were issued chemical warfare gear and sets of clothes for the desert. Then we were told to just always be ready.

We began making plans on what we should do. The next weekend I drove Kathy and the girls home to Moncks Corner. Kathy tried to talk with me about the deployment.

Kathy to the Rescue Part II

She tried to tell me how she would worry about me and how she did love me. I wasn't listening anymore. I would just answer shortly and kept saying I had to get right back to Florida because the call could come at anytime. We didn't even discuss the bills, and Kathy had no idea how I paid on some credit cards and then used them to pay other bills. Basically, I had to pay bills with bills just to get by. I didn't care if they got paid now or not.

About a week after I got back to Florida, they told us we would be getting the call at anytime. We were put on a two-hour leash. That means that from the time we got the call we had to be able to board the plane within two hours.

I'll never forget sitting in the living room alone and watching the first tracers shooting into the Iraqi sky on CNN. We were actually watching the start of war—live on television. I watched the first five minutes of the war and then the phone rang.

"Sergeant Stroud, implement your recall roster and notify the next person in the chain. Then, report to work with bags immediately."

Within twenty minutes I was at work, and within an hour the bus was carrying us with newly-issued M-16 rifles to Hurlburt Field to catch a C-5 cargo plane to fly us somewhere into the desert. The bus ride was stunningly quiet. Everyone was deep within themselves and the silence was eerie.

We joined many others on the flightline at Hurlburt and walked single file to the giant airplane. We took our seats, still in nearly complete silent reflection. The engines started, we taxied, and then rolled down the runway. As soon as the wheels lifted into the air the silence was broken by someone saying, "Here we come, *Saddam*, you better hide now."

The silence had been cut up and thrown out with laughter. Time for reflection had come and gone. We had no idea what to expect when we got there, and the attitude now was just, "Bring it on."

We never made it to the desert. We had flown about thirteen hours, then we felt the plane make a long, slow turn. It felt as if we had turned around. About four hours later we landed in England and lived in a hangar on cots for the next four months. We still don't know why we were there. We kept being told it was for a very important mission, but that mission never materialized, and we never left for the war zone. At first, we were not allowed to tell our families anything, except not to worry because we were not in the war zone.

I called my mother's house and she answered. I was relieved when she said Kathy wasn't there, and I gave Mom the message and hung up. I had made my decision of what I had to do, but I was not ready yet.

I called again about a week later. This was the first time we had even been allowed out of the hangar to work on the aircraft. This time Kathy was there.

We talked a little, and I was very short with my answers, and Kathy definitely knew something was wrong. It took her quite awhile, but she finally dragged it out of me.

"Kathy," I said, "I want a divorce."

There was stunned silence and then, "What..., no..., why?"

"We don't love each other anymore, and we don't have anything in common, and our life sucks and I want out!" I spilled my guts.

Kathy, crying now, said, "I can't believe this...I do love you...We are not getting a divorce."

"Yes, we are, good-bye," and I hung up the phone.

I did not plan to talk with Kathy again until I got back from this war. Then it would be to finalize the divorce. I was done, I didn't care. I could still see my daughters and help provide for them. The rest just didn't matter.

About a week later I got called into the first sergeant's office. I had no idea what he could be wanting with me. I hoped this wasn't about the poker we had been playing, because technically speaking, it was illegal in the Air Force.

"Stroud," he began, "what the hell is going on with you and your wife?"

"We're getting a divorce," I said. Now, I was kind of upset that he was sticking his nose where it didn't belong, but how did he know about this anyway?

"Look, your wife has been calling the squadron back home, and she has talked with the commander. She told him you just laid this on her over the phone, and now you won't call her."

"Well, I figured I have nothing more to say until I get home, and we get the divorce," I said defiantly.

"Oh, do you now?" Then his voice grew quite a bit louder. "Let me tell you what you are really going to do. You are going to get your ass on the phone and talk to your wife, do you understand me?"

"Yes."

"Then, you are going to call her at least every week until you get home. I don't care if you both decide you hate each others' guts and she tells you not to call. You are still to call her and let *her* refuse to talk to *you!* Now, get out of here!"

I had never had a chewing out like that before in my military career. I was mad, but I went straight to the phone and called home. Kathy answered on the first ring.

"What do you think you are doing?" I asked. "Why did you call the commander?"

"Because you won't talk to me," she replied.

"I don't have anything to talk to you about, I want a…"

"Kevin, you are going to shut up and listen to me, or I'll call the commander again and again. I swear I will. I have not eaten or slept in a week. I have cried the entire time. I've been sick to my stomach, throwing up, and I can't function. You cannot do this to me! To us! What did I do? Why are you doing this to me?"

Kathy was hysterical. I had never heard anyone sound the way she did. It scared me.

"Kathy, look at how we've been the last year. We've grown apart. Let's just start a new life where we can be happy," I said.

"I was happy. Kevin, I know it's been hard. I know I haven't been a good wife. I've just been too busy, too tired. I will do better, I promise!" She was hysterical and I couldn't listen anymore, it hurt.

"Kathy, I can't stay on this line now. We need to write. We won't talk about divorce anymore until I get back. Please eat."

"Okay, I will write to you, and please write to me. You will call next week, right?"

"Oh, yes," I said quickly, "I will definitely call every week."

I was still determined to get a divorce at that point. I just realized that the way I had gone about it was particularly cowardly. I would keep preparing her for what was going to eventually happen without forcing the issue right now.

Over the next few weeks, she wrote me every single day, and we talked each week. Soon, I began calling twice a week and I was writing more and more. I fell in love with her all over again. Our letters slowly grew into love letters that would make anyone blush. We missed each other. We were full of passion, full of love, full of life and of each other. We had not felt this way for such a long time.

When I did return home, Kathy had driven down to Eglin Air Force Base and met the plane. I went on leave, and Kathy and I took a small second honeymoon to the Epcot Center at Disneyworld. I have to say, it was even better the second time around.

After a few days, we went and got our girls and brought them back to Disneyworld. We had a great time as a family. Since Kathy couldn't figure out how I was paying the bills, she had arranged for a consolidation loan, and we had some leftover money for the first time in a long time.

As I said at the beginning, this is my one regret. Kathy had always been a wonderful wife. If I had managed money a little better, then she would not have had to work so hard with two little girls. She had supported me through years of school and stress from work. I had betrayed a trust so deep that it would take years to recover. When I threatened to break a vow (*til death do us part*) like that, she had been shocked. She never dreamed I would hurt her that way. I will never forgive myself for doing it.

She had fought harder for me than I ever thought anyone would fight for me. She had kept me from ruining my life forever when I was trying my best to destroy it. She stood her ground when most would have thrown up their hands in disgust and moved on. What a woman she is. She has saved me from myself at least twice now. Sometimes I feel she is my guardian angel, as well as my wife.

Oh, by the way, after we had fallen in love all over again through the mail and telephone, I got called into the first sergeant's office again. It seemed I had been accepted to Officer Training School, and I was to go home soon. It turned out we all went home soon.

I went from rock bottom to a brand new life within a few months of separation. Kathy had the strength and conviction to fight for me when I was being the biggest jerk imaginable. My hardened heart was softened. I listened, and my life turned around. Our debt issues were eased, and my dream of becoming an officer was going to come true. Very *lucky* indeed.

Miracle Seven
Emergency Leave

...and call upon me in the day of trouble; I will deliver you, and you will honor me.

—Psalm 50:15

I answered the phone and tried to sound as if I hadn't been in a deep sleep, even though it was 2:00 in the morning. Many of our relatives always *forgot* that Scotland was six hours ahead of them.

"Hello," I said, purposefully putting just a hint of annoyance in my voice.

"Kevin?" came the reply.

I couldn't quite place the voice yet, so I just said, "Yeah."

"Kevin, it's your Uncle Kirk calling you from the parking lot of Trident Hospital. It's pretty good this little cellular phone can reach clear over there to Scotland, isn't it?"

"Hey! Yeah it sure is," I replied truthfully. Cell phones were not yet in the hands of everyone as they are now.

I knew something was not right, though. Uncle Kirk doesn't call me, and he was just trying to give me time to wake up.

One Man's Miracles

"Listen," he said. "Your momma is not doing well. She had an infection, and it appears her kidneys are beginning to shut down. One has stopped and the other is only at about 18 percent. The doctor told us to get you on a plane."

I told Kirk what he needed to do. He had to tell the doctor to notify the Red Cross that this was an emergency, and I needed to get home. He must also tell them I am stationed at RAF Leuchars, Scotland, as an exchange officer.

Kathy and I sprung into action. I paused to shed a tear and be held by my wife, but I had to get packed. I thought I could wait until about 4:30 to call my commander to inform him. I doubted that I could get anything arranged by then anyway.

"What do you have to do, Kevin?" Kathy asked. "Can we go?"

"I don't think they'll pay for all of you. Well, um, yes, all of you come too, and we'll just have to pay for it."

Kathy got straight to packing for everyone. The girls helped with their stuff, but Kathy always had to give what they packed a once over, to ensure they got it right. She always found ten or twelve items the girls needed, but hadn't thought to pack.

I got on the phone and began calling for airline tickets, quickly finding out that last minute flights to the States were not cheap. The cheapest flight home was $1,650 per person. I knew the Air Force would pay for mine, but I didn't think they could pay for Kathy, Stephanie, and Jennifer. Our only option would be to put it on my credit card and try to get the Air Force Assistance Fund to give me an interest-free loan later. I got off the phone to talk with Kathy about the price, and see if she still wanted to go.

"Kevin, that's a lot of money," Kathy said. "Maybe we should wait and see."

Emergency Leave

Just then the phone rang. It was the Red Cross. They informed me there was an emergency with my mom, and that my presence was requested.

"How many are going?" the woman asked.

"Well, I guess I'm going to charge four, and hopefully get reimbursed for the price later for my ticket," I explained.

"No, sir. I will get your tickets and reserve them for you. You are authorized to take your entire family. What is the closest airport, and what time could you be there?"

I was totally impressed. It's well known that the Red Cross does good things for servicemen with emergencies back home, but this was way more than I expected.

"Glasgow is the closest international airport, and I'll need a couple hours notice to get my family there for the flight."

"OK, Captain Stroud. I'll call you back shortly."

It was somewhere around 3:00 A.M. Fifteen minutes after she hung up with me the same woman called back with four confirmed tickets flying from Glasgow to Charleston, South Carolina, and departing at 6:00 AM.

"Thank you! Thank you so much!" I said.

"No problem. You take care of that family of yours, have a safe flight, and I pray everything turns out OK," and she hung up.

As soon as I hung up the phone, it rang again. It was my commander informing me the Red Cross had called, and telling me to get home and take as much time as I needed. He told me not to worry about work, and he would see me when I got back. The Red Cross strikes again!

A half hour later we were on the road to Glasgow. With the layover in Newark, New Jersey, we arrived in Charleston at 9:00 A.M. that same day. From the time we left the house, we'd been traveling a little less than twelve hours. From my first call, my whole family was home in

One Man's Miracles

thirteen hours. The military and the Red Cross certainly take care of their own.

"How's Mom?" I asked my brother Rodney as we walked to the car at Charleston airport.

"Well, she is doing a little better actually. About an hour after we called, both of her kidneys were about gone. The doctor said there really was nothing more they could do. She had a massive infection from her open heart surgery, and they were battling the infection. They felt, however, that the kidneys were most likely too far gone, and when that last one completely shut down it wouldn't be long."

He continued, "Dad walked outside and fell to his knees and asked God to please save her."

"What?!" I asked. My dad has had a beef with God since his brother, my uncle, was murdered in a jail cell. He often said to me that if there is a god, then he is a jerk. Most of the time, he just denied God's existence. I'd prayed often for my dad to come to know Christ and ask for forgiveness, so maybe some good would come out of this ordeal.

"Yeah, he did. I couldn't believe it either. Well, about two hours later the nurse said her kidneys seemed to be responding a little."

I walked into my mom's room and gasped. My brother had begun to give me hope, and yet she looked horrible. She was so weak, she just moved her eyes to acknowledge my presence, and I leaned over and kissed her.

"Oh, she looks twice as good as she did a couple hours ago," my dad said. I'm glad I wasn't there to see that, because this was hard enough. The doctor came in shortly after that and said that one kidney was operating at about 20 percent and the other at about 15 percent.

The doctor gave this story its place in this book by saying, "It's *miraculous* the way her kidneys turned around like that." He added, "We're not totally out of the woods yet, but her odds are much, much better now."

Mom got better and better over the coming days. It appears she had had an infection for quite some time from the open heart surgery they had done months before. She also has a severe case of diabetes, and it always complicates healing. As the antibiotic got rid of the infection, her internal organs began working again. After two weeks it was time to take Mom home, and the nurse wheeled her out to the car.

"Well, Mrs. Stroud," she said, "you sure were *lucky*. Take care of yourself."

We stayed in Moncks Corner another ten days, and then the four of us headed back to Scotland. We sure were glad we were going back with greatly eased hearts.

Dad, by the way, was saved about seven years later. He had thanked God for taking care of his wife, but he felt his sins were just too great for Jesus to forgive. A friend of my brother explained to him one day that he was forgiven as soon as his confession was upon his lips. He knew he sinned; he praised the Lord for what he did for us all on that cross; and he praised him for rising again. He knew Jesus died so his blood could wash away all of our sins. He asked the Lord to fill his heart and take over his life—and he was saved. Praise God.

Mircale Eight
Katherine's Farewell

> Even though I walk through the valley of the shadow of death, I will fear no evil, for you are with me; your rod and your staff, they comfort me.
> —Psalm 23:4

As I relayed early in this book, I met Kathy when I was sixteen years old, on her fifteenth birthday. I stayed the summer between my junior and senior years of high school, and just called home one day and told my parents that I was staying in South Carolina. They tried to argue, but I was not going to budge no matter what they did, so they finally relented and I moved into a mobile home. Part of the time I lived with Kathy's brother, Larry. Part of the time I lived in the mobile home by myself.

Almost from the start, I was with Kathy every moment I could be with her. I stayed at her house quite a bit and I ate with the family at least once a day, sometimes every meal. Katherine always welcomed me and she trusted me with her daughter. She sometimes would think she needed to slow things down a bit, and she would try to limit our time together, but it never lasted more than a few days. Kathy and I would lie on her couch late into the night. Katherine had to get up and say, "That's enough, ya'll," before I would go home for the night.

Katherine had married at sixteen, and began having children shortly after. She had seven children, six boys, and the baby, a girl—my Kathy. One of her children had died in a car accident a couple years before I arrived on the scene. He was the middle child, and I know the entire family had taken Bobby's death hard because of the way they still talked about it. Katherine was one of the strongest women I had ever met. She could be gentle, loving, and understanding, but if anyone but family implied anything negative about a member of the Rhode family, they'd better watch out. Katherine fiercely protected her family and didn't let a grudge like that die down easily.

Katherine and I had a couple little spats along the way, but any family has those. I did not get a chance to thank her for all she did for me while dating her daughter and trying to live on my own during my senior year of high school. I don't think I ever really let her know just how much I loved her.

"Kevin," Larry said softly into the phone, "the doctors say it doesn't look good and Momma's kidneys are starting to fail. Let Kathy know and that she can call here to the hospital. I think ya'll better come down here."

I had retired from the Air Force just six months before and brought Katherine's daughter back to South Carolina after living around the world for twenty-four years. We had made a few trips down to Moncks Corner from the Clemson area, but planned to make more after we were settled.

Katherine's Farewell

Katherine had not been doing well for awhile now. Years of smoking had taken their toll, and she needed oxygen. Her back was in constant pain, and she had a recurring heart problem. She had been in and out of the hospital because they had been unable to keep fluid from building up in her lungs for very long.

I went and found Kathy in our bedroom. I told her what her brother had passed on to me. Her lip quivered just a trace as she looked up at me in silence. I hugged her, and then she was off to the phone. She wanted to talk with one of our sisters-in-law, Maxine or Sheila, as they would have the most information and pass it on to her. She got ahold of Maxine and spent the next forty-five minutes or so learning every detail about what was going on.

Because Maxine seemed more optimistic to Kathy, or because Kathy was struggling to accept the worst, she asked, "Maxine, do you think we should come now?"

"Kathy," Maxine said, "you can't put me in that position and I can't tell you to come or not to come, but your mother's kidneys *are* failing."

We arrived at the hospital about four hours later and found Katherine alert and able to communicate, but she was weak, and her kidneys had failed.

"Oh, ya'll came?" she said.

"Of course we came to be with you, Momma," Kathy replied.

"Well, I'm going to be all right," she said, but I believe she knew what was going to happen, and she didn't mean that she would be remaining with us here.

Kathy spent some time holding her mom's hand and looking into her eyes. I could tell that Kathy, who always had a great relationship with her mom, was struggling to figure out what she should say. We stayed at the hospital the rest of that night and watched Katherine sleep. She had been unconscious for quite some time, and although she would sometimes go wide-eyed, she would drop back off to sleep.

In the morning, Kathy and I decided to go to my mom's house to shower and take a quick nap because the doctors felt it would be awhile yet. We tried to take a nap, and I think I dozed off for a few minutes, but I spent most of the time resting and thinking of my mother-in-law. I prayed for her. I didn't pray for a recovery, but for God to wrap his arms around her and take her home as peacefully as possible. She deserved to leave her pain behind.

Later that afternoon, the whole clan was gathering. Katherine had not regained consciousness since shortly after we arrived last night. Everyone watched her, touched her, and whispered in her ear.

Soon, everyone in the immediate family was in the room: all of Katherine's sons' and her daughter's families, all the grandchildren, and even all the great grandchildren. At that time, Katherine opened her eyes, looked around and said, "What's wrong with ya'll?" She was conscious once more for a little while, and many got to touch her, and you could see the recognition in her eyes.

Soon, she knew her time with us was running out. She looked at us and said, "I love ya'll, each and every one. Bye-bye." Everyone in the room was now gathered closely around the bed, saying their last good-byes to a wonderful mother and grandmother. We cried, and some began telling her to go on to the Lord—that we would be OK, and she should just let go and go to Jesus. Katherine struggled to repeat herself a few times, and would even raise her arms and wave as she said, "Bye-bye."

After the last good-bye, she collapsed and never regained consciousness again. We watched in awe as she called out to Bobby, the son who had died, or other family members who had gone before her. Sometimes she reached out to someone we couldn't see, and I felt she had become very peaceful.

I knew that God had my mother-in-law, and though I knew I would miss her, I felt good for her. Her pain was being left behind, and she was going to a better place. Now I know many folks interpret what the Bible says about death in different ways. I believe you can find verses that seem to indicate the dead won't be raised until the second coming, and other verses that suggest your spirit will be with Christ. Although there are many that do, I don't even begin to suggest that I know what happens. All I know is that if Katherine was actually gathering with family members or not really doesn't matter. It doesn't matter if it's fact or a defense mechanism your mind invokes to ease the final moments of your life. Either way, it is a miracle. I believe she met with family and was led home. If not, she no longer had any sense of time, and she will be with Christ in the blink of an eye.

Kathy and I could not stay awake any longer, and at the urging of her brother, we went to my mom's again to get some sleep. The phone rang shortly after we fell asleep.

"Kevin," Larry said, "she's gone."

"Did she regain consciousness?" I asked.

"No. At the final moment she opened her eyes and sat straight up in the bed. She reached and said, '*Bobby!*' Then she was gone."

I choked up a little and both Larry and I said, "She's gone to a better place."

I don't know how anyone who witnessed her final moments in this world could possibly doubt the existence of God. The fact that she only regained consciousness to say good-bye during the few minutes when everyone was in the room. The fact (or the illusion, if you must) that Bobby, her dead son, came to lead her out of this world. *Lucky?*

Miracle Nine
Stephanie's Shocker

Then you will call, and the Lord will answer; you will cry for help, and he will say: Here am I.

—Isaiah 58:9

It was a normal Tuesday night and Stephanie, our sixteen-year-old daughter, ate dinner and watched a little television before bed. She was in high spirits and just her normal, beautiful self. We enjoyed each other's company, and later that night went to bed. All was good.

Just before midnight, Kathy and I were awakened by Stephanie moaning in the hallway. "Ooh, I'm sick," she whined. She whined in a voice that initially made us think she was purposefully overacting and being kind of funny. We chuckled a little, because how sick could she be when she was perfectly fine a few hours earlier? She went into the bathroom and began vomiting. Not able to make it to the toilet, her vomit landed in the first sink. After about a couple minutes and still vomiting, Kathy got up to check on her.

The spasms seemed to have passed, and Kathy began to clean the sink. "Stephanie," she said, "you can't throw up in a sink. Yuck, what a mess!" Stephanie, her place at the first sink now taken up with her mom, immediately vomited into the second sink. She then headed back to her bedroom, but slowly collapsed onto the hallway floor, still moaning in a mock childish voice. Okay, we thought, she is sick but still feels good enough to exaggerate a little—she even chuckled a little as she and Kathy discussed the need to vomit in the toilet as compared to the sink.

The next morning Stephanie was not any better. She now had diarrhea on top of the vomiting, and we felt sure she had a good case of the flu. She was also running a fever and Kathy made an appointment with our family doctor.

The doctor's visit was as expected. The nurse practitioner, Lisa, said it was most likely a virus, prescribed the usual clear liquid diet, and sent Stephanie home to let it run its course.

Stephanie continued to throw up and have diarrhea the whole day. Knowing she had to keep liquids in her to avoid dehydration, Kathy kept forcing them on her. The problem was that as soon as anything hit her stomach, she vomited. Late in the day the vomit changed to a very dark green liquid—bile. I went in to give her some oranges, because she thought she wanted them, and found the trash can was nearly a quarter of the way filled with this bile. This wasn't a small office trashcan, but a kitchen trashcan.

The next morning, her vomiting seemed a little less violent, and I headed off to work. Kathy was thinking if she wasn't better later in the day, she was going to take her back to the doctor. That morning, Lisa called. She said that she had thought about Stephanie all night, and though it was her day off, she wanted to check up on her. Kathy told her she was still very sick, very lethargic, and was throwing up lots of bile. Lisa said we should go ahead and bring her back in.

Stephanie's Shocker

Kathy went to get Stephanie dressed. As Stephanie raised her arms to put on a shirt, her undershirt lifted and Kathy saw a rash on her stomach.

A little while later, my cell phone rang with a message, because I must have been in a spot where the reception was disturbed. I checked the message and it was Kathy.

"Kevin," she said, "I'm at the doctor's office now and they are calling the ambulance over to take Stephanie to Oconee Memorial Hospital. Meet us there."

Something was wrong. The doctor's office is only a mile from the hospital, and for some reason they felt they needed an ambulance. I turned around and headed to the hospital. I was beginning to worry a little, but to calm my nerves I told myself she was probably just a bit dehydrated.

I arrived at the hospital just after Kathy and Stephanie. Kathy was at the counter doing the insurance paperwork, and she said I could go on back. I walked into the emergency room and into Stephanie's room. There was a doctor and four nurses in the room, all wearing masks and examining my daughter from head to toe. She was on an IV and looked very sick. The doctor came over and introduced himself and said the masks were a precaution in case Stephanie had spinal meningitis. He added, "Your daughter is very sick, and she is in a little bit of shock right now."

Kathy came in, and we stood in the corner and tried to stay out of the way as a team of folks worked quickly over our daughter. They could not get any blood out of her veins. She was in septic shock and the blood flow had stopped. The doctor struggled to get enough blood out of Stephanie's abdomen for the tests she desperately needed. We watched as a male nurse bent her into a fetal position and the doctor did a spinal tap. Memories of Jennifer's spinal tap as an infant, and the horrible scream that came from her little body, came flooding back to me. I was amazed

One Man's Miracles

that Stephanie did not even flinch. "This is pretty dry too," the doctor said.

After an hour or so the doctor came in and said everyone could take off their masks, because it wasn't meningitis. What a relief that was. He told Stephanie that he was going to have to do a check to see if she had left a tampon in, even though she said there wasn't. He checked and reported that there was no tampon in place and could most likely rule out toxic shock as well. He added again that our daughter was very sick. Her body had basically shut off all blood flow, except from the heart to the brain. He said her kidneys had shut down. All we could do was keep ruling things out as to what this could be. They had her on fluids and were aggressively treating her for all the major things it could be.

Kathy and I were hit with our first truck when he told us about her blood flow and her kidneys. Kathy's mother had recently passed away after her kidneys shut down.

Our family doctor came in and we talked to him about all we had seen. He said a few years ago he had been fooled by another young woman with toxic shock, and he felt strongly that we couldn't rule that out yet. He left us to find and confer with the emergency room doctor.

They took Stephanie for a CT scan to see if something was wrong with one of her organs. No problems noted.

Our doctor came back and said they were taking Stephanie up to ICU. They needed to put in a central line, because they had to get her blood pressure up with Dopamine. It was down to 60/26. We followed upstairs and were asked to wait outside until the central line was put in place.

Our doctor stayed with us and said, "I still feel strongly this is toxic shock, and we have started treating for that with antibiotics. The helicopter is on the way to take Stephanie to Greenville Memorial Pediatric ICU, because we do not have a pediatric unit here." Kathy and I were struck by truck number two as soon as we heard the helicopter was coming. He continued, "I want to assure you that I *think* we got it in time and I *think* she will make it." Kathy and I nearly collapsed with the force of truck number three.

The paramedics arrived from the helicopter, and we followed them as they rolled Stephanie out. Outside, the crew asked Kathy if she wanted to accompany them—a welcome surprise to both of us, since we had been told they don't allow other passengers. I kissed my little girl goodbye and told her that I loved her so much. I then sat in the ambulance and watched the helicopter lift her into the sky. I suddenly needed to get to my truck. I needed a moment alone. After it was out of sight, the ambulance took me to my truck and I climbed in the front seat. The tears began.

"Oh, God, please," I started as my cell phone rang. It was my brother Rodney, who had recently lost a son only slightly older than Stephanie. Since I had called Stephanie's grandparents when she went for a CT scan, I knew my brother was checking up on her. I had felt a horrible sense of loss for my nephew when he died and I tried to support my brother. I had told him that I could imagine how bad it is to lose a son. I know now that I was wrong. My world was crashing around me. I was helpless.

My brother had questions about how things were going and I tried to answer them. "Rodney," I started, but my voice cracked and hung. I couldn't breathe.

"Kevin? Kevin? Speak to me, Kevin!"

Forcing my cracking voice, I stated, "They just took Stephanie in the helicopter to Greenville!"

"Oh, God," he said. I later learned he had to pull over as Brandon's tragedy hit him again full force. He prayed, "Not another one of our kids, please."

Rodney somehow did get the message that the doctor said they thought she would make it, and he relayed that to Stephanie's grandparents, who were just a mess.

I forced myself to go home and get some things for the hospital—partly out of necessity for the items, but mostly because I wasn't ready yet for the forty-minute drive to Greenville. Stephanie's boyfriend called, and with a cracking voice of his own he inquired about her, and then asked if he could go with me. I told him I didn't think he would even be allowed to see her, and I wasn't coming home for a while, maybe not for days. He said, "I don't care, I just want to be close." I couldn't refuse.

The drive was mostly silent. I just couldn't hold a conversation with Jon. My thoughts were on Stephanie, and "what-if" she didn't make it. I'd look at the trees flying by and think I would have to slam into some of those. Then I'd think about my oldest daughter, Jennifer, and my parents, and my brother's family, and my friends, and realized I wouldn't be able to do that. Working again would just be out of the question. We'd downscale to my military retirement and just sit there until I could join my daughter. Very dark thoughts took over me and threatened to take me down. My world had changed forever.

By the time I got to the hospital, her kidneys had begun to barely work again and Dopamine had raised her blood pressure. They had pumped ten liters of fluid into her to "jump start" her kidneys. Trouble with breathing because of the excess fluid accumulating in her lungs was to come next. They knew it was coming and warned us they might have to put her on a respirator and maybe even dialysis.

As test results came back, they became more and more sure it was toxic shock. I received calls from various people that first night and there must have been at least

Stephanie's Shocker

six churches praying for Stephanie, and three prayer lines implemented.

There was very little sleep that first night. The nurse, a complete professional, was constantly in and out of the room. I was thoroughly impressed by this angel from heaven, and now I don't even know her name. The next morning, she was still there when I awoke from a short doze and she said, "It's amazing! It is just amazing how fast her kidneys have come back. They are almost back to normal. It's amazing!" I counted three "amazings" in that exchange, and that was before she even talked with Kathy. It felt as if at least one of those trucks had been lifted off of me.

Stephanie spent the next five days in Pediatric ICU, and each day showed improvement. The doctors had prepared us for a long recovery. Two days later, Stephanie came home, and three days after that returned to school. This sickness that can take over a healthy child and kill her in three days had left her body, and she recovered quicker than anyone had indicated she would.

While it was an "amazing" recovery, it really wasn't surprising. We had a lot of people praying for Stephanie. God answered.

While I had heard of toxic shock in the late seventies, I really didn't think it was a problem anymore. In the days that followed, I heard numerous stories—a girl who died, a sister who lost a foot, a cousin who lost an arm. It seems toxic shock is again on the rise, most likely because of the new "super absorbent" tampons. I keep hearing how *lucky* Stephanie is, and I agree. Lucky the nurse practitioner just couldn't get her out of her mind and called on her day off. A few more hours and Stephanie would not have lived. Lucky that a lot of people cared and prayed for her and God intervened. Lucky that all of the nurses and doctors involved cared and treated her with complete professionalism.

Thank you to all those professionals. Thank you to all the folks who prayed. Most importantly, thank you, Lord!

Stephanie showed me the following paper about six months after I first wrote this book. Understandably, some of her facts of that experience are somewhat confused, but the power of the same experience from her point of view justifies it being here in this book. There are other miracles here that, while I didn't recognize them then, or even realize they had happened, they definitely impacted my life.

A Shocking Experience
By
Stephanie Sloan

It seems like a bad experience is always looked back on with an understanding that it happened for a good reason, and that reason changed the outcome for the better. What happened to me was something that only happens to 1-17 of every 100,000 women. Why did it happen to me? I don't know, but I do know that it helped me get over certain struggles in my life at the time.

It all started in February 2005 in the middle of the night. The night before I was absolutely fine. My parents, my boyfriend, and I were eating dinner and watching a movie. My boyfriend went home and I went to sleep. I woke up with a start and felt a sudden urge to throw up. I struggled to get up, because for some reason my body felt stiff and heavy. After I finally got out of my room, I started down the hallway. When I got about halfway to the bathroom I felt extremely dizzy and slowly collapsed on the floor, as if gravity had decided to pull extra hard on my body. I was helpless to get up, so I used what strength I had to call out to my mom down the hall. At first the situation was funny,

Stephanie's Shocker

me being stuck flat as a pancake on the floor in the middle of the night. So I wasn't too surprised when my parents told me from their bedroom to stop joking around. I cried out again, and my mom got up to see what was wrong. She helped me up to the bathroom, where I could not help but throw up in the sink. It was either the sink or the floor, since I couldn't hold it down in time to reach the toilet.

My mom held my hair back, saying, "Oh, no, not the sink!"

Looking back now, it seems quite comical. Especially since after I filled up the first sink, I moved to the next sink and puked some more, while my mom was gagging and trying to clean out the first. I stopped throwing up for a minute, while my mom helped me over to the toilet just in case I got the floor next time.

I had never thrown up so much in my life before that night, and the few days following. I puked over and over again, until all that came out was thick, putrid, green, and slimy bile. I eventually got back in bed, though I didn't sleep. I had a tall trash can next to me that I hung over all night. My mom brought me some water, but as soon as I swallowed, it just came back up along with some more bile.

In the morning my mother and I went to our family doctor. My body had become so stiff that I could hardly move to change clothes, get to the car, and walk into the building. I had visited the doctor a lot around that time, for I had been going through depression and anorexia. I had gotten over the anorexia, but the depression stuck with me, and worsened since my cousin died not long before I had this sickening experience. I honestly wouldn't have cared less if my life had just ended at that point. But fate obviously didn't have that in store for me.

The doctor's first thought was that I had a stomach virus and should come back in a couple of days. So we went home, and my body started aching all over and was getting worse every second. The next morning my mom had to help me undress, because I couldn't move my arms and neck. When she lifted my shirt she saw a red, blotchy rash on my stomach. We wondered what this could be, for it could not have been just some ordinary stomach virus.

When my mom was getting ready to go back to the doctor, we heard the phone ring. It was the doctor on her day off work, calling to tell us that she had been up all night pondering what was wrong with me. She said she had a feeling that something more serious was wrong, and that I should come back up there immediately.

While in the doctor's office, I realized I was having trouble breathing and comprehending what people were saying. Everything was happening so fast, and my body began to shake violently. The doctors tried to take a sample of my blood, but to no avail, for my veins were so thin and were not flowing very much blood. Next thing I knew I was being put on a stretcher and being rushed to Oconee Memorial Hospital in an ambulance. When I got there I was rushed to an emergency room where everything seemed to be spinning fast. Doctors were everywhere, and I couldn't move a muscle while they poked and pricked for blood that wasn't there. Then they had to do an examination. What a horrible experience it was to have a room full of people and my parents at the doorway freaking out, while a woman gave me a pelvic examination. After she deduced that nothing was wrong with that, they gave me a spinal tap. Spinal taps are proved to make a grown man cry, which shows how much pain I must have already been in when they did it to me, because I barely flinched. Three people had to hold me down though, because my shaking had become so bad that I was bouncing on the cold, hard table. My body was

Stephanie's Shocker

going into shock. I faintly heard a man tell my dad that he *thinks* I'll make it.

I was told later that I was sent to Greenville Hospital by helicopter because Oconee Memorial didn't have a pediatric intensive care unit. I remember being put on another stretcher, but do not remember being taken anywhere on it. The only thing I do remember about the ride was a man's face looking down on me, telling me to stay with him. The next thing I remember was being put on a hospital bed and being uncomfortable from the stiffness of my body. It felt like every pressure point on my body was burning. Within minutes I developed bedsores, because my body's systems were shutting down and my only blood flow was from my heart to my brain. Again my body felt as if gravity was pulling it down extra hard upon the bed that felt like burning coal against my limbs. They had to get blood, so they took it from a huge IV line in my neck, from which they also administered all sorts of medicines and vitamins. One of the doctors recognized my symptoms from a case of toxic shock syndrome that he or she had dealt with a while back. So now we knew the name of my sudden sickness.

The blood work came back revealing that my kidneys had completely shut down. This was a surprise to me, because I didn't feel any pain near my kidneys. I wondered how long they were shut down before I got there. All we could do now was wait and see if I got better from the enormous amount of medicine being pumped into my body. The medicine was the only thing keeping my heart beating. My feet and my hands were stone cold and blue. Nurses had to turn me over to wash my back and to ease my back sores.

I thought I was going to die. My life wasn't flashing before my eyes, but I did look back on all the painful times in my life up until then. Times like when I threw up at my friend's house, because I was forced to eat during the time that I was anorexic, when I screamed at God for making me feel so depressed all the time and for hating myself every second of the day, and when I stood over an open coffin that was holding my closest cousin. These were the memories that made me not care if I died, and if they were my only memories I probably would have. However, the memories that gave me hope to live were much more powerful. Like when I became friends with a boy who always knew how to make be laugh even when I was depressed and on the verge of committing suicide, and when that same boy came rushing to the hospital when my sister called about my sickness, and when he skipped three days of school to stay overnight in a waiting room chair so that he could be with me. I also thought about my parents being so worried about me when I was starving myself, and when I was going to a therapist for depression. What really kept me motivated to live was when I heard my dad tell my mom that when he called my uncle to tell him what happened to me, my uncle had to pull over on the road he was driving on, because he had started to cry. The thought of me dying caused him to think of his son that just died, my cousin.

My dad reported that my uncle had said, "Oh, no, not another one of our babies."

Though the prospect of going to heaven and seeing my cousin again seemed really great at the time, I was determined to live. I couldn't allow two deaths in the family to happen in the same year. So it was good news when another blood sample told the doctor that my kidneys were up and running again, something that the doctors said was the fastest kidney recovery they had ever seen. They told my parents that I was lucky, because most people who get TSS end up losing a part of their body from lack of oxygen. He also said that I came extremely close to dying, and that if I had waited any longer to go to the doctor I most likely would have.

I was in the hospital for two weeks recovering, and each day felt better than the last. The first time I stood since being there felt like the first time ever in my life. I was dizzy, but a nurse helped me along until I could stand and walk by myself. Then came the day I was released home to rest for a few days before going back to school.

I look back on that experience with joy, because it made me realize that I had so much to live for. It helped me through the death of my cousin, because I always felt his presence next to me. Bad times in life always happen for a reason, as well as the good times. This experience was a pivotal time in my life, because from then on I stopped thinking of my own feelings before the feelings of others. I realized that even though I didn't particularly love myself at the time, my family and friends did love me. That kind of love is always worth living for.

Miracle Ten

This Book

The LORD will fulfill his purpose for me; your love, O LORD, endures forever—do not abandon the works of your hands.
—Psalm 138:8

I have always been a reader, according to my mother. From the time I could first read, I have always been reading something: comic books, Hardy Boys, adventures, magazines, cereal boxes, et cetera. I've dreamed of publishing a book since I first graduated from high school in 1980.

While in Germany, with the Air Force between 1982 and 1987, I worked pretty hard toward that goal. I was attending college and was particularly focused on my English and creative writing classes. Fellow students in my creative writing class always told me that I was talented and could be the next Stephen King. Mr. King was newer on the scene and a particular favorite with the students.

I began writing a novel and short stories. I sent the short stories to many, many publishers and began collecting my piles of rejection letters. I was in my early twenties, and I was extremely proud when I received my first handwritten rejection from an editor. A handwritten rejection means you got very close to getting your story published. The rejection said I was a talented writer, but a bit too male chauvinistic in my approach. I found this ironic, as this rejection came from the female editor of one of the popular men's magazines. Just bear in mind that I was young and desperate for a published work, and believe me when I say I would never write such a piece again.

Between work, school, and fatherhood, I gave up on my dream of writing, or at least put it on hold. As my pastor says, *life got in the way*. I did finally get published while in the Air Force for a piece I was asked to do for an Air Force magazine on my work and deployment with the B-2 bombers during Operation Iraqi Freedom, but I really don't feel that counts. I just didn't have the time to follow a dream of full-time writing. I just didn't have time for a lot of things. Once I retired from the Air Force and went into real estate, I still didn't have time because now, for the first time in my life, I didn't know where my next payday was coming from, and I had quite a pile of bills.

When we first returned to upstate South Carolina at my retirement, Kathy and I decided it was time to try and find a church. To be honest, it was initially more because I figured it would help my real estate business than for any Christian sense of duty or strong desire for church. Since I already relayed that I was saved in the early 1980s, this might be a surprise to you.

After my salvation, I became somewhat disillusioned with churches. The missionary church that I was part of largely taught salvation and the second coming of Christ. They used real world events and convinced you the second coming was imminent. Oh, how I looked forward to that day (and still do by the way). But after a year and Christ still hadn't come, I became discouraged with the church. Then, after I missed three consecutive Sundays, I received a letter

This Book

from the church leadership that said if Kathy and I didn't contact them and let them know why we had missed those Sundays, they would be forced to remove us from the church roles. The final straw had come. After numerous "Hell and Damnation" services as a kid, and this invasion on my life by my church, I felt there was no need for church.

I had a relationship with *my* Christ, and I knew I was a baby in *my* new Christian life. I would no longer let a church tell me what my relationship with *my* God had to be. I took a class in religion in college, and I found that most of the world religions had a common thread. I could not believe, for example, that some other Christian denominations, as that missionary church had taught, were the Great Satan and were deceiving millions to their eternal death. I did a paper on Dietrich Bonhoeffer and his "Religionless Christianity." A lot of what he said appealed to me at the time, and I have since grown in Christ to know that a non-denominational, multi-racial Christian church is what's right for *me*.

So Kathy and I visited a large Baptist church and found its atmosphere just didn't seem right for us. The next Sunday, we decided to check out a little place in a funny igloo-looking building that was called the Tri-County Worship Center. From the moment I walked in the front door this church seemed to be a place I would like to go. Modern, Christian, multi-racial, and so friendly we could hardly believe it. Most of the church members were on a mission trip to Peru, so we made it a point to come back the next week and check it out. The next week just confirmed what we already felt—this was our new church.

Okay, the background necessary to explain this chapter is in place. I have always dreamed of being a writer. I have not had enough time for quite some time to write, for my family, or to even attempt to do anything for God. I had found a church that for the first time in my life made me feel somewhat cheated when I have to miss a Sunday.

My first year anniversary in real estate had arrived. I had done it, I was still in a business where somewhere in the neighborhood of 80 percent of first year rookies will fail. God was providing for me. You see, God and I had a deal that I prayed about and imagined he accepted. If he would just give me the business I needed to get myself out of debt, then I could and would begin to tithe to the church, and I would be able to take more time to do something like the mission trip to Peru. I really did want to go to Peru with the church, but I just didn't have time.

I made more money than I would have if I had stayed in the military, and except for a couple short months in the winter, I was able to pay my bills and even pay a couple smaller credit cards off. Unfortunately, things kept coming up, like new bills for things that were needed—college, repairs, and the list goes on. I had to charge more items, and I ended up that year exactly where I started on my debt, but at least I was paying the bills just fine.

It was around this time that Stephanie was almost taken from me as discussed in a previous chapter. I needed more time, and I needed to stop working all the time. The one thing about real estate—your phone better be ringing, no matter what time of day or day of the week.

I decided to move out of the office and begin to work at home. This was a big step, as it meant I would no longer get floor duty. Floor duty is when you are at the office and you get all of the incoming calls or walk-ins to the office.

This Book

The first few months of this arrangement were working great. I had much more time around the house, though it was still very difficult to leave my cell phone for any length of time. Still, I found myself sleeping a lot later and relaxing on my couch a lot more. I had time—maybe not quality time because I was still chained to my cell phone—but at least I had time.

"Russ," I started on a call to my broker, "you know since I moved out of the office my income has increased, but I'm finding myself with extra time on my hands."

"That's good, but I know after twenty something years in the Air Force, you are not used to having that kind of time," he said.

"You're right. I'm sitting around too much. I'm thinking about buying into a home inspection franchise with my brother. We'd surely be busy getting it off the ground, but I'm sure I'd still have time to focus on lake property. I've been considering moving out of house sales anyway and only marketing land."

"Well, Kevin, there is no problem in that as far as we are concerned. You would, of course, have to disclose you are licensed with us whenever you are hired to inspect one of our listings, but there are no other concerns."

"Great, Russ. I'm in the final stages of investigating this, and I want to move quickly when I decide. I appreciate your time. Bye."

I hung up, relieved to hear the company had no problem with me expanding into another aspect of real estate. Everything seemed right about this business venture. I only had to find a way to get the $35,000 that I needed to start up and get rid of the gut feeling that I didn't really want to do this. I kept thinking that after retiring from the Air Force this time commitment was something that I really didn't want. This was not even considering the fact that I would be creating considerably more debt in an effort to get out of debt. On the other hand, it would provide a more stable income flow that should increase my disposable income enough to finally make progress on lowering my debts.

The next morning was Sunday and Kathy and I headed off to our church. As we entered the building, I saw Bo standing off to the side. Bo and I seemed to hit it off, and I looked forward to talking with him. He's an appraiser and became the first choice whenever someone asked me to recommend one. He's knowledgeable, a leader in the church, and a good man.

I talked a little with Bo about my idea to move into home inspection. He agreed with me that it was booming business right then. We had arrived kind of late and saw we only had thirty seconds to the start of the service, so we excused ourselves and quickly found our seats.

The service began with its usual modern worship music. I really enjoy the music played in our church, but today I kept thinking about this business possibility. I was at church, where I wanted to be, but my mind surely wasn't all there.

Pastor Tracy said that today's message was going to be about freedom to worship. He said, "Worship comes in many ways, not just music, because let's face it, not everyone can sing, and not everyone can play an instrument. Worship comes in the form of the building of these walls, in the work you do for God, in so many countless ways. Here is one form of worship that I want you to sit back and enjoy."

The pastor was replaced with one of our younger members who struggled onto the stage, hunched over like an old man with a cane. The incredible song, "*I Can Only Imagine*," began to play.

> *I can only imagine what it will be like,*
> *when I walk by Your side...*
> *I can only imagine, what my eyes will see,*
> *when Your Face is before me!*
> *I can only imagine, I can only imagine.*

The conversation I'd had with my eighty-year-old father-in-law just a couple of weeks earlier came flooding back to me. Kathy's mom had passed away about six months earlier. Years of smoking had taken their toll, and she suffered in the last years. Her entire family was by her side in the hospital the last time she was conscious. Hilly and Katherine were married fifty-six years, and it was hard on him to let her go. We all cried when Katherine passed away, but we all knew she was in a much better place and no longer suffering.

Well, a couple of weeks ago Hilly and I were sitting alone in his living room as he was inhaling deeply on his breathing medicine, because years of smoking had also gotten to him. He began to cry and said, "Kevin, I'm eighty years old, and I don't know why the Lord is keeping me here!"

I didn't know what to say. Here was a man I will always remember as the strong farmer who worked in the fields from first daylight to darkness. The knowledgeable man who took me fishing and always complained to me that I needed to be getting my family to church.

Now I saw him in the young performer on the stage as he struggled around the stage worshiping his Lord and trying to imagine being with him.

One Man's Miracles

> *Surrounded by your Glory, what will my heart feel?*
> *Will I dance for you Jesus? Or in awe of You, be still?*
> *Will I stand in Your presence, or to my knees will I fall?*
> *Will I sing 'Hallelujah!'? Will I be able to speak at all?*
> *I can only imagine! I can only imagine.*

On the first verse, the actor was my father-in-law. He did his best and struggled mightily to worship as he imagined. He just wobbled as he tried to dance. He slowly tried to crouch to his knees, but couldn't quite make it.

On the second verse, my father-in-law was able to throw away that cane and stand completely erect. He danced like a young man and threw himself to his knees in front of his Lord. Hilly was stronger and more limber than ever.

A few tears ran down my cheek. My throat hurt as I fought to hold back my emotions. My father-in-law's suffering will come to an end soon. His Lord will take care of him in paradise.

All of my thoughts of some business venture had disappeared. My heart was completely open to any message from the Lord. I was focused on my praise for our Lord and what he had to say to me that day.

Pastor Tracy's message that day was about how you can get freedom in worship. It was about how you can be free of nervousness to raise your hands in the chapel, or say a "praise God" to a complete stranger. He said people who were ashamed or nervous to worship the Lord had probably never had an encounter with God. Not to say they hadn't been saved, for that is completely different. But they had not experienced a life-changing encounter with God.

He asked with heads bowed, "Who among you wants to seek an encounter with God?" My hand went up as he said, "Amen, amen, God bless you."

He then asked the congregation to stand and join hands. He said he saw many, many hands all across the congregation go up and many wished to have the type of encounter with God that would change their lives. We prayed, and I felt the familiar tingle I get whenever I'm open to the Holy Spirit. So far, that sensation had only come to me while at church. It flowed from me into the hands I was holding as I prayed for each person next to me to have the encounter he or she might seek.

The service ended and we headed out to eat our Sunday meal. I told Kathy I saw her dad in that performance, and that it had brought tears to my eyes.

I prayed often during the next week for my encounter. I looked for it in everything I did. Driving down the road, I kept my eyes not just on the road, but scanned for anything that could be my encounter.

Friday morning came, and I had not had any encounter with God. It had been a pretty slow week, although I was booked up for Saturday with showings. My phone began ringing about 10:00 A.M., and I talked with four or five new prospects who were looking for waterfront property. Some wanted land and some wanted homes, and they all ranged in value from $350,000 to $850,000. Three of them wanted to look at things on Saturday, but I was already booked up.

Now I am happy to have four or five clients of that magnitude in the entire summer. To have the possibility of that many in one weekend is just mind boggling. A sales commission on that much real estate is likely to be in the $80,000 range. If I were to get that kind of business in one weekend I could surely pay off all my debts, not counting my house. *Could this be my encounter?* But I felt this just couldn't be the encounter I was searching for, because I was unable to meet with them. Some said they would call later to reschedule, but in all likelihood they moved on to other real estate agents.

The week ended and it was Sunday morning again. Kathy had left for Texas on Thursday for the funeral of her Aunt Joyce, her mom's sister. I really didn't feel like going to church by myself today and besides, I had an open house scheduled in the afternoon. I decided I wouldn't go to church, as I had gotten up late anyway.

I did my morning routine and sat down and watched some news. I was now awake and feeling much better. I was really feeling that I needed to go to church, but I just didn't want to go by myself. I watched a little more television and looked at the clock. It seemed to be moving slowly this morning. I still had an hour before church. As the feeling that I needed to go could not be shaken, I finally decided to go and got ready.

Pastor Tracy began his message after some great new music was performed and sung by all. "Today, we finish up on our freedom series and I'm going to talk to you about freedom in Christ, and how it begins with tithing."

Oh..., I came for this today. I know I need to tithe, and I really want to, but I just can't afford it until I pay off my bills. God and I have an agreement.

"Now I know a lot of you are saying, *Oh, here we go again, the preacher is going to tell us we need to give more money*," Pastor Tracy continued.

Pastor Tracy went on and gave a good message about our need to tithe. We need to give not just money, but time, skills, et cetera. I had heard all of it before, and I already knew the passages in the Bible that show the need to tithe. I know the churches do God's work, and they can't survive if everyone only gave a dollar a week. I know I need to do God's work and I want to, and I will just as soon as I get debts paid down and I can have the time to do it. I know

This Book

that in the book of Malachi we are told to test God—the only time we are told to test God. I know, I know, I know.

I left church that day glad I went to church, but feeling a little disappointed. Why had I been unable to shake the *need* to go to church today by myself when I just didn't feel like it? It had been a tough two weeks, because I did not get my life-changing encounter with God, and now I didn't even get the message I had begun to feel I was meant to get today.

As I pulled into my driveway, I had something going on in my thinking. There was a thought spinning around up there, as if I were missing something. It was fluttering around and I could feel it was important. I put my Expedition in park and it came to me. It started as a trickle and then, BAM!

> *I have time now, I've complained about having too much. I've been making good money but not making progress on my debts—My way is not working. God has been putting in my heart that I should write for him. In the last week even an idea has come to me—One Man's Miracles. I've always wanted to write. My father-in-law focused me and opened my heart to hear last week's message. I sought an encounter. I received more calls in one day from clients searching for values that would have easily paid off my debts. God can pay off my debts in a moment, and that is not the problem. I can be working for God by tithing. I need to tithe my income as well as my time. I do have the time now. God wants me to write for him and help my church to do its mission by tithing. If I just do what God asks me to do, everything will be taken care of in my life.*

My body was tingling as these thoughts came rushing to me. Not the usual tingle I sometimes feel in church, but much stronger and much more sustained. I knew, like I've never known anything in my life, what I had to do. God had revealed his plan and how events of the last year had brought me closer to God so I would seek him more. How events of the last two weeks came to this exciting conclusion.

I had danced around the house, getting a few things for the open house I was holding that afternoon. I laughed out loud and thought how magnificent and intricate the events in my life have been to get me here. I got back into my car and cranked up the local Christian music station. The first song's chorus came on, and while not an exact quote it was something like, *"You know what you need to do. You can now spread your wings and soar!"*

I looked down at my arms and saw the goose bumps all over them. My entire body was flooded with the Holy Spirit. I danced as I drove down the road with my windows down and Christian music blaring. I raised my hand to God, yelling numerous times out my car window, "Praise God!" Anyone who knew me as the quiet and reserved fellow I usually am would probably have thought I'd gone completely nuts. For the first time ever, I felt totally wrapped in the arms of Jesus. It feels so good, I never want to leave again.

I thought about my conversation with Russ and the home inspection franchise. Just how stupid could I be? I wanted time, I got it, so now I was seeking a way to fill it with a new business? I felt better than I had ever felt in my life. Today, as I write this first draft, two days since my life-changing encounter with God, I am still tingling with excitement and getting goose bumps numerous times throughout the day. I am still realizing parts of God's work to get me here. Like how it was necessary that I go to church by myself that day. Kathy had to have gone away at just that time. God needed me alone, so I could find him.

This Book

The song, *I Can Only Imagine,* is a great song and definitely one of my personal favorites. But after the feelings I've been having the last two days, and while writing this, I have to say—you can't even imagine! Praise God and God bless you!

Miracle Eleven

Salvation

Everyone who calls on the name of the Lord will be saved.

—Romans 10:13

It was 1982 and I wanted so much to go to Alaska. I've always been an outdoors guy and the fishing, hunting, and hiking in the Alaskan wilderness greatly appealed to me. I was so happy when my orders arrived to Elmendorf Air Force Base in Anchorage, Alaska. It wasn't to last long.

The next day, I received the cancellation of those dream orders and a set of new orders to Germany. I was brokenhearted, and it took me quite some time to get excited about my new assignment.

As it turned out, I was so very "lucky." In Alaska, I would have been busy every weekend, and surely would not have thought about church. Germany, however, and the language barrier, caused us to seek activities with Americans, which led to us finding a small missionary church. As you'll see, if not for the *luck* of a change in assignments, four people may not have found Christ and could very well still be lost in the wilderness.

While the other miracles sort of follow a chronological order, I chose to put this chapter last, because all the others helped either to lead me to Christ in the first place, or caused me to grow in him. I believe everyone goes through a Christian life and hence the term *born again*. The stages of a Christian life may vary greatly in regards to their length or the turbulence that results, and it depends on the individual and where Christ desires to lead him or her. I also know that the Lord will never give up on you and will succeed in leading you where you are to go.

So why does this chapter belong in the book? First of all, the Bible says that to be saved you must believe in the greatest miracle of all, that Jesus allowed himself to be beaten, humiliated, and hung on that cross to accept the punishment for our sins. Then after his death and entombment, Jesus rose again three days later. I don't think anyone who believes can attribute that to *luck*. Secondly, as I reflect on my life since I accepted Christ, I can recognize the distinct stages in my Christian life, just as we have stages in our regular life. Our maturity in Christ moves from the infant stage, to the child stage, to the teenage stage, to the young adult stage, and finally to the mature Christian adult. Reflecting back on these stages, I realize how the events of my life have led me to this point. I am growing in Christ and I can now recognize his hand in all I do. That is truly a miracle.

Infant Stage

Kathy and I were living an exciting life in Germany. When we arrived in the country, Kathy was only eighteen and I was twenty. We were happily married, but were also growing up together. We were never heavy drinkers, but we enjoyed using alcohol on occasion and since we had no

Salvation

children at the time, we enjoyed partying a bit with friends. Germany, after all, is the land of beer and wine.

We experienced the Oktoberfest in Munich and the Wine Fest in Bad Durkheim. Basically, everyone gets drunk and runs around riding rides and hitting each other with little toy squeaky hammers. By the way, large glasses of wine and swinging or spinning carnival rides don't mix very well. To this day I struggle when forced to ride one of those swinging ships. Not usually a ride you get sick on, but the memories of the Wine Fest come back in a flash. I don't think any kind of ride had ever gotten me so sick.

Money was beginning to get a little better. Kathy worked and I made staff sergeant my first time testing. We had enough to take care of our needs and go out and have a good time, though we didn't have enough to travel Europe as much as we would have liked.

Some people say we missed out on a lot getting married so young, but I've never thought that was the case. We just had the experiences together, both good and bad. We were young, in love, and overseas—what were we missing out on?

We knew, however, that something was missing in our lives. We were very frustrated that we hadn't been able to have a child, for one thing. We had begun to go to a missionary church in Sembach, Germany, and we went a couple times each month. We did go enough to hear the message of salvation, and we picked up the free literature. After a couple of months, I knelt alone on the floor of our living room and prayed to God. That prayer went something like this:

Jesus, I really don't know how to do this and I don't want to recite a prayer I read on the back of a leaflet. I know I've prayed to you a few times, but in general I have been a sinner and I really don't feel worthy to talk to you. I know I believe in you, Lord. I love you for what you did. You suffered and allowed yourself to be hung on a cross. I know you did it for me, as unworthy as I am, to be cleansed of my sins. Lord, the Bible says all I have to do is accept this gift and I do Lord. I ask that you come into my life and guide me. Lord, I am weak, so very weak and I cannot follow you alone. Please, Lord, take control of my life and lead me where you want me to go.

Later that day, I told Kathy that I had been saved. She was interested and asked me how I knew. I showed her the literature again and we talked about what it took to know you were going to heaven one day. We knelt together and prayed together for the Lord to come into her life as well, and praised him for our salvation.

I then began trying to go to church much more regularly. I bought books and read, studied, and highlighted the Bible, and talked with knowledgeable people about Jesus and the Bible. Besides salvation, the main message of the missionary church was the second coming of Jesus. I especially liked a comic book the church bookstore had about things in this world and how they tied in with the prophecies of the Bible. I was convinced that the coming of Jesus Christ back to earth was imminent.

I kept trying to get more and more information. I wanted to learn. I needed to know what I was supposed to be doing. I was excited in my salvation and I wanted to find what God wanted of me. I went on temporary duty to Spain shortly after that and talked with anyone I could find about God. I was very shy about my relationship with Jesus and would never yet talk with someone about religion unless they started it. Thank God there are a lot of recognizable

Christians out there, so all I had to do was say, "Hi," and a conversation seemed to ensue.

I had never realized something until I wrote this chapter and I decided to leave it right here where it was revealed to me. Another of those *coincidences* happened in my life at this time. I looked at my old baptism certificate which I keep in my Bible. It is dated November 1983, and Jennifer was born May 24, 1984. If we go back nine months, it means Jennifer was conceived sometime in late August. I returned from Spain in late October and wanted to be baptized, which we did November 22, 1983. This means that it was sometime between May 1983 and July 1983 when I had knelt in my living room and received God's gift of salvation. Kathy and I had tried to have a baby for over three years and she conceived within weeks of our salvation! Now, that's a *coincidence!*

CHILD STAGE

Our baptism is where I became a child in my Christian life. I had gained enough knowledge to feel somewhat comfortable talking about Christianity. I knew I wanted to follow Jesus and baptism was my first step. As I said previously, Kathy and I took that first step together in 1983.

I found a friend in Christ at work. Chris was young guy who, while about the same physical age, was a little older than I was in Christ. He knew a little more, was a little more comfortable expressing himself, and he had a couple more experiences to share with me. We sometimes spent hours talking about Christian subjects and beliefs. We would sometimes argue about beliefs and then turn to the Bible to settle it.

I also talked with our close friends, Gary and Elke. Within a couple of weeks, I was kneeling with them in a back room of a church, witnessing their acceptance of the Lord's gift of salvation.

This stage was still mainly characterized with gaining knowledge, albeit a deeper knowledge. I took a couple religion classes in college, tried to start Bible study at the church, and bought a study Bible and began studying the background of certain events and/or scriptures in the Bible. I found it fascinating that the vast majority of the world's religions were so similar. I began to be troubled when a certain denomination condemned another denomination. The literature was plentiful where it did just that. Who were we to condemn people? Each denomination felt its faith was based just as much on the Bible as another. As I looked at scripture, I could understand the differences. Maybe God speaks in different ways to different folks.

I felt the knowledge I was gaining was bringing me closer to Christ, but further away from the church that led me to him. I began to miss a week here and a week there. It was a pretty long drive to the church from the housing area where we lived, and I was thinking about trying to find a new church that felt more right for me.

The letter I received, saying that if I wasn't at church the next week and had a satisfactory explanation as to why I had missed a number of services, angered me. When I talked to the pastor about it, and he questioned if I had indeed "achieved" salvation, I entered the next stage of my Christian life.

Teenage Stage

I became rebellious to the church. Not rebellious against God at this point, but I refused to go to church. As

Salvation

I looked around, I saw hypocritical church members often condemning someone for something while they did the same thing or something else certainly comparable. In the southern states of America where I am from, I remembered all-white churches or the all-black churches where members of the other race were definitely not welcome, although no one would "officially" state it. I saw famous television evangelists being guilty of adultery and committing embezzlement scams. Church, it seemed to me, was surely a corrupt way to find Jesus.

I also became disappointed that the second coming my church had talked so much about had not happened. I was disappointed that my life after being saved did not become supernaturally easier somehow. Slowly, I began to doubt everything. Again, some people told me that this meant I was not really saved—that I somehow hadn't really believed in my heart what I was saying. Of course, I knew better than that. I had believed and truthfully asked for the Lord's help. I had asked him to guide me and to help this weak man to do his will.

Slowly, more and more doubts crept in. I continued to talk with God, and my rebellion against him (having doubts) was very short lived. I prayed and was constantly amazed how often my prayers were answered. I had a relationship with Jesus. A personal one where he was part of my life and had his arms wrapped around me.

I came to a point where I only really talked to God when I needed something. I really didn't have much time for him. I had problems in this world that I had to address, and I felt God really didn't have anything to do with the major part of my life.

I guess you could say I was inattentive. One moment, I'd feel Jesus and think I was on the right track and the next moment it would be weeks before I even thought of Him.

Still, every time I prayed for an assignment, a promotion, a grade in school, or even Officer Training School, God came through for me and I thanked him.

I remained in this stage for a long time, frankly until about three years ago. This means from 1985 until late 2004 I remained a child in Christ. There is little doubt that it was mainly because of my rebellion against churches. I now understand that a church is a group of Christians gathered together to do God's work. Some churches will be right for some people and other churches right for others. One thing for sure, however: no church is perfect. Churches are made up of people and there is no one person currently on this earth who is perfect. Every one of us has sinned and will surely sin again, and God gave his only son so that even though we are weak, we can have everlasting life.

I began to go visit churches as a way to improve my real estate business, but instead I found a church home that just felt right. Going to that church, coupled with Miracles 7, 8, and 9 of this book, have finally moved me into the next stage of my Christian life.

Young Adulthood

I am now secure in my relationship with my Savior. I understand that he accomplishes so much through us, and we need to be willing to work for him. I know I have to come to grips with issues like money and tithing, time, family and friends, et cetera. I now know I need to work these things out, and I genuinely want to do that. I pray that I will become a valuable tool for the Lord.

I've realized churches, although imperfect, do a lot of the work for the Lord. They cannot operate without money. The Bible says one tenth of your income is his, and if you are using it then you are stealing from him. The church needs that money, and if everyone tithed as they are supposed to, this world would surely be a much better place. It's not about being able to afford it. It's about *faith* that God will take care of you.

I've realized time is an asset that God needs you to tithe as well. If everyone gave one tenth of their time to God, we could accomplish a whole lot of his work. If you just don't have time, then you are too busy. Again, it's about *faith* that God will take care of you.

Family and friends are important to us and important to God as well. I realize, though, that you cannot use your family and friends as an excuse. God must come first in our lives. When you put him first, everything else will be taken care of for us. Again, it's about *faith* that God will take care of you.

I believe *when* I get these issues worked out, then I will make the transition to the next stage.

Mature Christian

You can tell a mature Christian when you see one. It is apparent in his or her actions and words that he is a follower of Christ. While still imperfect, mature Christians are comfortable in their relationship with the Lord and have their priorities right. Through their actions, both in and out of their church, they do God's work and know that everything else is taken care of for them.

I believe at this stage you have to be careful not to become a fat, lazy Christian. So comfortable in your relationship that you forget others need your help and that you really don't have all the answers. You must continue to seek and listen to God.

Recognizing the paths and stages that your life has taken, and seeing how God has led you, is an amazing thing. Every time you detoured, God gently led you back. It took a long time for the Lord to get me to the next level, because I was pig-headed and believed my relationship with God was somehow different. God never gave up on me, though. I could feel God jump for joy when my mind finally opened to see what God was doing in my life. He had tried to get through to me for a long time, and I finally listened.

I pray that those reading this book realize that miracles are happening all around them. I pray they take the time to reflect on their lives by taking a close look at where they are now and what events in their lives got them there. Did they answer God's call? Or have they refused to answer, and certain events in their lives are, or were, God's further attempts to get their attention? God is working in your life, you can believe that. He is trying to make you understand that he is here, he loves you, and he wants you to be with him forever. What a miracle! Praise God! Amen.

To order additional copies of this title call:
1-877-421-READ (7323)
or please visit our Web site at
www.pleasantwordbooks.com

If you enjoyed this quality custom-published book,
drop by our Web site for more books and information.

www.winepressgroup.com
"Your partner in custom publishing."